GRAMMAR ESSENTIALS

GRAMMAR ESSENTIALS

Third Edition

NEW YORK

Published in the United States by LearningExpress, LLC, New York.

Library of Congress Cataloging-in-Publication Data
Grammar essentials—3rd ed.
p. cm.
Rev. ed. of: Grammar essentials / Judith F. Olson, 2nd ed. c2000.
ISBN 1-57685-541-4
1. English language—Grammar—Handbooks, manuals, etc.
I. LearningExpress (Organization) II. Title.
PE1112.O43 2006
428.2—dc22

2006000600

Printed in the United States of America
9 8 7 6 5 4 3 2 1
Third Edition

For information on LearningExpress, other LearningExpress products, or bulk sales, please call or write to us at:

LearningExpress
55 Broadway
8th Floor
New York, NY 10006

Or visit us at:

www.learnatest.com

CONTENTS

INTRODUCTION

How to Use This Book

Writing is a lot like playing the piano. Some people enjoy it more than others, and people who are good at it study and practice it. No one is born playing the piano, but anyone can do it if he or she wants. The same goes for writing. If you're interested in learning about writing and in becoming a better writer, this book will help you demystify and acquire the coveted power of the pen.

This book covers the basics of writing: punctuation, usage, and diction. There's no fluff here; this book is for busy people who want to learn as much as they can as efficiently as possible. In 20 chapters, each of which you can complete in 20 minutes, you can improve your grasp of grammar. Each chapter contains a Grammar IQ Quiz, lots of examples that illustrate the grammatical rules, and plenty of opportunities for you to practice the skills.

Many people are afraid of writing. They look at a blank sheet of paper or an empty computer screen and say, "I just don't know what to write. Even when I know what I want to say, I'm afraid it will come out looking wrong and sounding stupid."

But writing has three distinct advantages over speaking.

1. **You can take it back.** Although writing is not instant communication and it doesn't allow for immediate response and exchange, written communication can be retracted. Once words are spoken, you can never unspeak them. However, writing can be revised until you've written the exact words in the exact tone you want. It's a more careful, thoughtful way of communicating.
2. **You can make it clear.** The second advantage is that writing forces you to clarify your thoughts. If you're having trouble writing, it's usually because you're not yet finished with the thinking part. Sometimes, just sitting down and writing whatever is on your mind helps you discover and organize what you think.
3. **It lasts.** Another advantage is permanence. Ideas presented in writing carry far more weight than spoken ideas. Additionally, these ideas can be reviewed and referred to in their exact, original form. Spoken ideas rely upon the sometimes inaccurate memories of other people.

Writing is nothing more than carefully considered thoughts on paper. Many great ideas and observations are never born because their creators don't express them. You may have some wonderful concepts inside your head with no way to get them out where others can see them. This book can help you express your ideas.

Develop your own plan for completing the 20 chapters in this book. They're designed to be completed in 20 minutes a day, but you may want to take more or less time with each lesson—or more time with chapters you find difficult and less with those you know cold. You could do a chapter each weekday and come out with a better knowledge of grammar in only a month. Or you may want to do more or fewer chapters at a time. You should, however, plan to complete at least two chapters a week. If you leave too much time between lessons, you'll forget what you've learned.

By the time you finish this book, you'll have much more confidence in your writing, and you'll probably be a better thinker. If you practice what you've learned, it won't take long for other people to notice the new and improved you.

GRAMMAR ESSENTIALS

CHAPTER 1 GRAMMAR IQ QUIZ

Which of the following sentences would be more appropriate in a business communication? The answers and explanations follow the quiz.

1a. Josh is wishy-washy.
1b. Josh is indecisive.

2a. It was agreed upon by the editorial department that Maria would lead all meetings with the design team for the purpose of avoiding a "too many cooks spoil the broth" situation.
2b. In order to avoid confusion, the editorial department delegated Maria to lead all meetings with the design team.

3a. Your supervisor informed the CEO that you do not support the company's spending plans for the upcoming fiscal year.
3b. The CEO has been informed by your supervisor that you are not on board with the spending plans that have been made for the company's upcoming fiscal year.

4a. It has been discussed at great length by the board members that vacation time be increased from two weeks to three for employees who have been with the company for three years.
4b. The board members have seriously discussed increasing vacation time from two weeks to three for employees who have been with the company for three years.

5a. We have been referring to this policy.
5b. This is the policy to which we have been referring.

Answers

1b. is the better choice because the language is less colloquial.
2b. is the better choice because it is written in the active voice, and is less wordy and colloquial.
3a. is the better choice because it is written in the active voice, is less wordy, and contains no colloquialisms.
4b. is a better choice because it states the idea more clearly using fewer words, and uses the active voice.
5a. is a better choice because it is not wordy.

CHAPTER

1

THE RIGHT WAY TO WRITE

Sometimes, the words we use when we speak aren't effective when we use them in writing. This chapter discusses the difference between spoken and written English, informal language, wordiness, and precise language.

Grammar concepts to know:

- **colloquial** [ka LOW kwee 'l], **colloquialism** [ka LOW kwee 'l izm]—an informal word or phrase used in conversation, but not appropriate for business communication or other formal writing
- **active voice**—a sentence in which the subject (underlined) is performing the action of the verb (John read the letter.)
- **passive voice**—a sentence in which the subject (underlined) receives the action of the verb (The letter was read by John.)

Written language makes a permanent impression, one that can't be changed by rephrasing the words the way you can in a conversation. That's why it's important to think carefully before you write. Take a look at the note on the following page. What kind of an impression will it make?

Manny,

Got your note today. Thought I'd get right back to you. Keep you from getting in a tizzy about this whole moving thing. It's still kinda early to pack stuff for the move cause the new building isn't even done yet. Might as well wait til it is.

Seems like Jack has been chosen by the top dogs to head up the entire moving process with all its various aspects. Due to the fact that he hasn't started doing a thing yet, there's no sense in the rest of us getting panicky about it. Don't freak out; it'll get done.

J.C.

SPOKEN ENGLISH VERSUS WRITTEN ENGLISH

Many of the speaking patterns we use are not suitable in business writing. For example, if you listen to a conversation, you might hear incomplete sentences, sudden subject changes, or abbreviated versions of words and phrases. Although these expressions are common in casual conversation, they are confusing and inappropriate when you are writing to a customer, supervisor, or employer. Avoid these things in written communication.

Incomplete Sentences

Quite often, we use fragments when we speak. We count on our tone of voice and our expression or the reaction of the listener to fill in the spaces. In writing, this isn't possible, so it's important to write complete sentences that express complete thoughts. See Chapter 3 to learn how to avoid sentence fragments.

Sudden Subject Changes

In everyday conversation, we switch subjects easily. Two speakers can exchange far more information in two minutes than a reader can absorb in the same time period. That's why it's important to use the reader's time efficiently. Switching subjects requires time and mental energy. Write everything you have to say about one subject before moving on to the next. Link subjects together to make it easier for a reader to go from one idea to another. See Chapter 15 on making subjects agree with verbs.

Abbreviated Words

Many words we use in conversation are not used when we write. Following is a list of words frequently used in speech; however, the written versions are different.

Spoken Version	**Written Version**
cause, cuz	because
coulda	could have
gonna	going to
hafta	have to
kinda	kind of
shoulda	should have
sorta	sort of
til	until
wanna	want to
woulda	would have

Symbols instead of Words

Don't use symbols in place of words, even if it seems simpler or more efficient. Write out the complete word in any written communication if you want to be taken seriously.

four (not *4*)
to, too, two (not *2*)
and (not &)
extra (not *x-tra*)

COLLOQUIALISMS [ka • LOW • kwee • 'l • izmz]

Colloquialisms are informal words and phrases such as *in a bind, pulled it off, real good,* etc. These words and phrases are widely used in conversations between friends, but in business writing, they portray an attitude of familiarity that may cause your message to be taken less seriously than you intended or even insult your reader. A friendly, colloquial tone is fine in a personal letter; however, a more formal tone is better for business communication. Compare the following paragraphs. If you received these two memos from your employees, which would you take more seriously?

> We're really in a bind on our end. Seems like every time we turn around something else comes up. Today was one of those days. A few

of the guys who decided to live it up last night couldn't get over it this morning. Since we were shorthanded, we didn't come close to our daily quota. This is really ticking me off.

We're having trouble meeting our quota as new problems keep arising. Today was a difficult day because several employees who stayed out late last night were unable to make it to work on time. Because we were shorthanded, we missed our quota. This is extremely upsetting.

The following sets of sentences illustrate the difference between colloquial and standard diction. The colloquial sentences in the first column are rewritten in the second column using more standard language.

Colloquial	**Standard**
The car works real good.	The car works **well**.
Ben got sick of waiting.	Ben **tired** of waiting.
I'm awful thirsty.	I'm **very** (or **quite** or **extremely**) thirsty.
It looks like they'll be late.	It looks **as if** (or **as though**) they'll be late.
The cake was real good.	The cake was **very** (or **quite**) good.
We're in a bind.	We're in **trouble**.
Drew put it off till tomorrow.	Drew **postponed** it until tomorrow.
I don't have that much of a chance.	I don't have **a very good** chance.
Rosa got there in time.	Rosa **arrived** in time.
Jill got the order.	Jill **received** the order.
I like to pal around with her.	I like to **spend time** with her.
Kip got the wrong idea across.	Kip **conveyed** the wrong idea.
I just don't get it.	I just don't **understand**.
How come you're leaving?	**Why** are you leaving?
What for?	**Why**?
I see where you're coming from.	I **understand your point**.
Leah had one of those days.	Leah had a **difficult** day.
Rodney can't make up his mind.	Rodney can't **decide**.
Robin will keep an eye on things.	Robin will **watch** things.
They're going to live it up tonight.	They're going to **celebrate** tonight.
The Knicks pulled it off.	The Knicks **succeeded**.

WORDINESS

Not only do extra words waste space and time, but they may also distort the message or make it difficult to understand. Get in the habit of streamlining your writing, making your sentences as concise as possible. If you use five words where three would do, delete the extra words or structure your sentences to avoid them. Read the following examples.

Wordy: It was a twenty-minute period of time after the accident had occurred when the emergency vehicles arrived to lend assistance. [21 words]
Revised: The emergency vehicles arrived twenty minutes after the accident. [9 words]

Wordy: It was decided that the club would organize a committee for the purpose of conducting a search for a new chairperson. [21 words]
Revised: The club organized a committee to search for a new chairperson. [11 words]

The additional words add no information. All they do is take up space.

Buzzwords and Fluff

Buzzwords are words that sound important but don't add much meaning to writing. They include words such as *aspect, element, factor, scope, situation, type, kind,* and *forms.* Fluff words such as *absolutely, definitely, really, very, important, significant, current, major, quite,* etc., also may add length to a sentence, but like buzzwords, they seldom add meaning.

Wordy: The nature of the scheduling system is a very important matter that can definitely have a really significant impact on the morale aspect of an employee's attitude. Aspects of our current scheduling policy make it absolutely necessary that we undergo a significant change.
Revised: The scheduling system can affect employee morale. Our policy needs to be changed.

Wordy Phrases

The following table lists several phrases that can be reduced to one or two words.

Wordy	Concise
puzzling in nature	puzzling
of a peculiar kind	peculiar
at this point in time	now, today
at that point in time	then
regardless of the fact that	although
due to the fact that	because
in order to	to
by means of	by
of an indefinite nature	indefinite
exhibits a tendency to	tends to
concerning the matter of	about
in connection with	with
in the event that	if
in relation to	with

Some wordiness is created by using the passive voice. In the **active voice**, the subject of a sentence is the source of the action in the sentence. In the **passive voice**, the subject receives the action.

Passive: Jeff and Dara were rejected by the board because they did not meet all of the requirements outlined in the guidelines.
Active: The board rejected Jeff and Dara because they did not meet all of the requirements outlined in the guidelines.

Passive: The non-profit agency was not given funds by the foundation this year due to a lack of private donations.
Active: Due to a lack of private donations, the foundation did not give the non-profit agency any funds this year.

Writers sometimes stretch their sentences by using unnecessary words. The following table illustrates stretched sentences rewritten to be more concise.

Stretched Sentence	Concise Sentence
Alex seems to be impatient.	Alex seems impatient.
We must know what it is that we are doing.	We must know what we're doing.
These requests will be considered by us on an individual basis.	We'll consider these requests individually.
The musicians, who were distressed, left the hall.	The distressed musicians left the hall.
There are new problems arising daily.	New problems arise daily.
Due to the fact that we were early, we found great seats.	We came early and found great seats.
The consideration given in the latest evaluation is an example of how I was treated unfairly.	My last evaluation was not fair.

PRECISE LANGUAGE

Work to make your writing as precise as possible. In doing so, you will communicate your meaning more effectively while using fewer words. In other words, you will make your writing more concise. Choose words to help you transmit an exact meaning.

Imprecise	Precise
Homer managed the project.	Homer organized the staff and monitored their progress.
Melody doesn't handle people well.	Melody yells at and insults coworkers.
Richard can relate to Patty.	Richard understands Patty's position.
This is a good proposal.	This proposal explains the problem and suggests a solution.
These bad instructions confused me.	These disorganized, vague instructions left me with no idea how to fix the stool.
We had a nice time with you.	We enjoyed eating, chatting, and swimming at your house.
I always have trouble with this machine.	I can never get this truck started.
I like to have fun at the company picnic.	I like to eat, mingle, and play games at the company picnic.
We need to clean up before we go.	We need to put away the supplies and shower before we go.

REVIEW

Remember the memo at the beginning of this chapter? Go back and read it again. Try to rewrite it by revising colloquial and informal language, eliminating wordiness, and using precise language. You can do this in many ways. Then turn back to this page and read the memo below as an example of one way of rewriting it.

> Dear Manny,
>
> I'm replying to your note about packing to move to the new building. Jack is in charge of organizing the entire process. However, since the building is not yet finished, he hasn't started the process yet. I'm sure that if we're patient, everything will turn out fine. Don't worry. I'll let you know as soon as Jack begins work on the move.
>
> J.C.

CHAPTER 2 GRAMMAR IQ QUIZ

Tell whether the following sentences are compound or complex. Answers and explanations follow the quiz.

1. After I peeled the potatoes, Marcus cut them into small pieces for the stew.
2. I ordered the cheesecake, and Toya ordered the ice cream sundae.
3. Erika designed the house, and Paul furnished it.
4. Every time I hear that song, I think of my birthday party.
5. I wanted to go swimming, but Alec preferred to play tennis.

Answers

1. complex—the sentence contains a dependent clause (*After I peeled the potatoes*) and an independent clause (*Marcus cut them into small pieces for the stew*).
2. compound—the sentence contains two independent clauses (*I ordered the cheesecake. Toya ordered the ice cream sundae.*).
3. compound—the sentence contains two independent clauses (*Erika designed the house. Paul furnished it.*).
4. complex—the sentence contains a dependent clause (*Every time I hear that song*) and an independent clause (*I think of my birthday party*).
5. compound—the sentence contains two independent clauses (*I wanted to go swimming. Alec preferred to play tennis.*).

CHAPTER

WHAT *IS* A SENTENCE, ANYWAY?

This chapter teaches you about the basic unit of communication in the English language: the sentence. Mastering this chapter will give you the key to mastering everything else in this book—and in your writing!

Grammar concepts to know:

- **subject**—the part of a sentence that names the person, thing, or idea
- **predicate**—the part of a sentence that contains "the verb that tells"
- **clause**—a groups of words with a subject and a predicate
- **independent clause**—a clause that can stand alone and express a complete thought
- **dependent clause**—a clause that needs an independent clause to complete its meaning
- **complex sentence**—a sentence containing an independent clause and a dependent clause
- **compound sentence**—a sentence containing two or more independent clauses

A sentence is the basic unit of thought in the English language. This chapter will help you learn to write a complete, coherent sentence.

THE PARTS OF A SENTENCE

A sentence has both a subject and a predicate and expresses a complete thought. For example, read the following.

The snow is falling.

This is a sentence because it names a thing (snow) and tells us something about it (that it is falling). It also expresses a complete thought.

The Subject

The part of the sentence that names the person, thing, or idea is called the **subject**. The subject can be one word or several words. The **complete subject** consists of the person, thing, or idea and all of its modifiers, such as adjectives and adverbs. The complete subjects are highlighted in each of the following sentences.

A loud argument broke out at the game.
The young, worried pilot read the storm warning.
The newspaper article mentioned our newest menu item.

Every complete subject contains a **simple subject.** The simple subject, which is a noun or pronoun, is the most important word in the complete subject. It is the word that names the person, thing, or idea the sentence is about. Look at the complete subjects highlighted in the previous sentences. Which word is the most important in each complete subject? The simple subjects are highlighted below.

A loud **argument**
The worried, young **pilot**
The newspaper **article**

Practice

Read the following sentences. In each one, underline the complete subject. Then circle the simple subject, or the person, thing, or idea the sentence is about. At the end of the chapter, you will find the complete subjects, with the simple subjects in bold.

1. My severe stomachache seemed better at the doctor's office.
2. Our new mail carrier slipped on the ice this morning.
3. The longest, dreariest road lies between the Nebraska borders.

The Predicate

The part of the sentence that contains the verb that explains something about the subject is called the **predicate.** The predicate can be one word or several words. The **complete predicate** consists of the verb and all of its modifiers. The complete predicates are highlighted in each of the following sentences.

A loud argument **broke out at the game**.
The young, worried pilot **read the storm warning**.
The newspaper article **mentioned our newest menu item**.
Mrs. Dawson **is our most difficult customer**.
My neighbor **rarely complains about snow**.

Every complete predicate also contains a **simple predicate**, or verb. The simple predicate is the word that shows action or helps to make a statement about the subject. Look at the complete predicates highlighted in the sentences above. Which word shows action or helps to make the statement about the subject? The simple predicates are highlighted below.

broke out at the game
read the storm warning
mentioned our newest menu item
is our most difficult customer
rarely **complains** about snow

Practice

Read the following sentences. In each one, underline the complete predicate. Then circle the simple predicate, or the word that shows action or helps to make a statement about the subject. At the end of the chapter, you will find the complete predicates, with the simple predicates in bold.

4. The purple curtain ripped at the seams.
5. Our president always buys some of our competitor's products.
6. Dotted print backgrounds are difficult to read.

COMPOUND SUBJECTS AND PREDICATES

A sentence can have more than one subject joined by *and, or,* or *nor* that shares the same verb. This is called a **compound subject**. The compound subjects are highlighted in the following examples.

Horace and **Beth** both asked for a promotion.
Hannah and **Terri** are the shift supervisors in this department.

A sentence can also have a **compound predicate:** more than one simple predicate that shares the same subject. The predicates may be joined by *and*, *or*, or *nor*.

Dimitri **wrote** a letter and **sent** it to the personnel department.
Horace **called** his supervisor and **asked** for a meeting.

CLAUSES

Like sentences, **clauses** are groups of words that have a subject and a predicate. Clauses are either **independent** or **dependent**.

Independent Clauses

Independent clauses are groups of words in a sentence that can stand alone, because they express a complete thought. The **simple sentence** consists of one independent clause:

The snow is falling.

Sometimes, more than one independent clause is included in the same sentence, which is known as a **compound sentence.** When this happens, the clauses are separated by a comma and a **conjunction**, or joining word (*and, but, or, for, nor, so, yet*). The independent clauses are underlined in the following sentences.

I gave her good advice, and she took it.
My dentist pulled my wisdom teeth, but it didn't hurt as badly as I thought it would.
I don't like brussels sprouts, and my sister doesn't either.

Dependent Clauses

Dependent clauses, also known as **subordinate clauses**, are groups of words in a sentence that have a subject and predicate but can't stand alone because they don't express a complete thought. They are dependent on independent clauses.

When I saw the snow was falling

An independent clause can complete the thought:

When I saw the snow falling, I went to get my snow shovel.

Sometimes, sentences are made up of one independent clause and one or more dependent clauses. These are known as **complex sentences.** In the following sentence, the independent clause is in bold and the dependent clause is underlined.

I put on my heavy coat when I saw the snow was falling.

Practice

Underline the independent clauses in the following sentences. Check your work with the answers that follow.

7. Believing that the pages were in the right order, I mailed the manuscript.
8. Even though I couldn't afford the house anymore, I wanted to renew my lease on it.
9. Whenever the weather forecasters predict rain, the sun shines.
10. In the box sitting underneath the desk, I found my hat.
11. I called Tom again, and the new programs finally arrived.
12. I went for a walk today, and I mailed your letter.

Answers

1. My severe **stomachache**
2. Our new mail **carrier**
3. The longest, dreariest **road**
4. **ripped** at the seams
5. always **buys** some of our competitor's products
6. **are** difficult to read
7. Believing that the pages were in the right order, I mailed the manuscript.
8. Even though I couldn't afford the house anymore, I wanted to renew my lease on it.
9. Whenever the weather forecasters predict rain, the sun shines.
10. In the box sitting underneath the desk, I found my hat.
11. I called Tom again, and the new programs finally arrived.
12. I went for a walk today, and I mailed your letter.

CHAPTER 3 GRAMMAR IQ QUIZ

Determine whether the following groups of words are sentences or fragments. Answers and explanations follow the quiz.

1. Across the street.
2. Stringing her new tennis racquet.
3. A small studio with a view of the park.
4. Ori received the highest grade on the math final.
5. Although it had already started to rain.

Answers

1. fragment—the group of words contains neither a subject nor a verb.
2. fragment—the group of words contains no subject.
3. fragment—the group of words contains no verb.
4. sentence—the group of words contains a subject (*Ori*) and a verb (*received*).
5. fragment—although the group of words contains a subject (*it*) and a verb (*had started*), the word *Although* makes it a dependent clause that does not express a complete thought.

CHAPTER

FILLING OUT SENTENCE FRAGMENTS

Don't stop. Before the sentence is done. Sentence fragments—incomplete sentences—are popular tools for advertisers, but they have no place in your writing for work or school. By the time you finish this chapter, you'll be able to recognize and correct incomplete sentences in your writing.

Grammar concepts to know:

- **fragment**—a group of words, punctuated as a sentence, that does not express a complete thought
- **subordinating conjunction**—a joining word that creates a dependent clause

In the English language, we write in complete sentences because they accurately communicate our ideas. A well-written sentence leaves little room for confusion. The memo on the following page is nearly impossible to understand because the writer uses incomplete sentences, or **sentence fragments**, rather than complete sentences. Bob has no idea what Bart needs.

Bob,

Can't get this to work. Think it's got something wrong with the alternator. Been a problem already. You remember. Can you fix this? Need it before the convention next week.

Bart

REVIEW

In the last chapter, you learned that independent clauses can stand alone, while dependent clauses can't stand alone because they do not express a complete thought. Sometimes, dependent clauses are mistakenly used in the place of complete sentences. When this happens, they are considered sentence fragments. Any group of words that is punctuated as a sentence but does not express a complete thought is called a **sentence fragment**.

DEPENDENT CLAUSES AS SENTENCE FRAGMENTS

A dependent, or subordinate, clause cannot stand by itself as a sentence; it needs an independent clause to support it. Read the following groups of words. Even though they contain a subject and a verb, their meaning is incomplete. The subject in each dependent clause is in bold, and the verb is underlined.

Before **we** went on to the next project
Whenever this **company** changes its policies
If the **road** is too icy for traffic

Read the following examples carefully. They illustrate the difference between an independent clause and a dependent clause. The subjects are highlighted and the verbs are underlined in each example.

I left an hour later than normal. (Independent clause: sentence)
If **I** left an hour later than normal (Dependent clause: fragment)

When our **group** finished its report (Dependent clause: fragment)
Our **group** finished its report. (Independent clause: sentence)

Whenever **Rita** tried to explain herself (Dependent clause: fragment)
Rita tried to explain herself. (Independent clause: sentence)

Subordinating Conjunctions

Again, read the previous examples carefully. Notice that each dependent clause is longer than the independent clause. The groups of words are the same, but the dependent clauses have an extra word at the beginning. These words are called **subordinating conjunctions**, because they modify a dependent, or subordinate, clause in some way; and join it with a dependent clause.

If a group of words that would normally be a complete sentence is preceded by a subordinating conjunction, something more is needed to complete the thought. In the sentences that follow, each of those fragments has been rewritten to express a complete thought. Notice that each sentence now has both an independent and a dependent clause. The dependent clauses are in bold and the independent clauses are underlined in each sentence.

If I left an hour later than normal, <u>I missed my favorite talk show</u>.
When our group finished its report, <u>we left for lunch</u>.
Whenever Rita tried to explain herself, <u>she confused her words</u>.

Here is a list of some of the words that can be used as subordinating conjunctions:

after	*if*	*though*	*where*
although	*once*	*unless*	*wherever*
as	*since*	*until*	*while*
because	*than*	*when*	
before	*that*	*whenever*	

Sometimes, a subordinating conjunction is a phrase rather than a single word:

as if she could read my mind
as though he had been playing for years
as long as he can figure this out
as soon as they get here
even though it is getting dark
in order to learn another language
so that you can spend a semester abroad

Make complete sentences out of the following fragments by adding an independent clause to each subordinate clause:

When the mayor runs for re-election,

Although it seems complicated,
While I was doing my homework,

PHRASES AS SENTENCE FRAGMENTS

Dependent clauses are only one type of sentence fragment. Read the following word groups. In each pair choose the group of words that expresses a complete thought. The other group of words in each pair is a fragment. See if you notice any similarities among the groups of words that are fragments.

The class was ready for the next step.
According to the teacher.

Watching the sky.
The picnickers saw the air show.

Visiting for the first time in years.
I greeted my grandmother.

Emily sat on the sofa.
Wondering what to do next.

These fragments are made up of **phrases**: groups of words that do not contain a subject or a predicate and do not complete a thought. Combining the two sets of words in each pair will make one complete sentence. With some of the word pairs, only a comma is needed. With others, a few extra words must be added to incorporate the phrase into the rest of the sentence. The following examples demonstrate how this is done.

According to the teacher, the class was ready for the next step.
Watching the sky, the picnickers saw the air show.
Since she was visiting for the first time in years, I greeted my grandmother.
Emily sat on the sofa, wondering what to do next.

Practice

Combine the following word pairs into a complete sentence. Check your work with the corrected sentences at the end of the chapter. Often, there is more than one way to combine the word groups.

1. The next train will be arriving. Five minutes from now.
2. Not liking it one bit. Jane ate the casserole.
3. They used a fog machine to create the effect of smoke. One from an Army surplus store.
4. Send your news on letterhead stationery. To represent your company.
5. Not long before the last witness had testified. The judge ran out of patience.

Separated Fragments

Sometimes, a fragment is part of a complete sentence, but it is written as a separate sentence. Read each of the following word groups. In each pair, one is a complete sentence; the other is a fragment. See if you can decide which word group expresses a complete thought.

The fans drove all over the downtown area.
And looked for a parking spot.

And noticed an old classmate in the crowd scene.
We saw the movie.

Faulty equipment and poor workmanship.
They refused to pay the bill in full.

In the pond outside our building.
Canadian geese have built a nest.

The following set of words in bold represent a complete sentence. Combining the two sets of words in each pair makes both sets part of a complete sentence. Try combining the examples yourself.

The fans drove all over the downtown area.
And looked for a parking spot.

And noticed an old classmate in the crowd scene.
We saw the movie.

Faulty equipment and poor workmanship.
They refused to pay the bill in full.

In the pond outside our building.
Canadian geese have built a nest.

Combined Sentences

There's more than one way to combine sentences, but here's one.

> The fans drove all over the downtown area and looked for a parking spot.
> We saw the movie and noticed an old classmate in the crowd scene.
> They refused to pay the bill in full because of faulty equipment and poor workmanship.
> In the pond outside our building, Canadian geese have built a nest.

REVIEW

Read each of the following word groups. If the word group is a sentence, identify the subject(s) and the verb(s). If the word group is a fragment, think of a way to make it into a complete sentence. Check your work with the answers at the end of the chapter.

6. Wishing he were almost anywhere else.
7. In the end, it made no difference at all.
8. That camping outside would be fun.
9. Before the part stops working completely.
10. The unidentified man looked like a reporter.

Go back to Bart's memo at the beginning of the chapter. Here are the facts concerning Bart's situation.

- Bart is part of the grounds crew for a convention center.
- Bart regularly uses a riding lawn mower.
- The mower broke down three weeks ago.
- Bob sent the mower to be fixed.
- The alternator was replaced with a rebuilt one.
- The biggest event of the year is scheduled to begin in eight days.
- The grounds need to look "perfect."
- Bart needs a working mower to do his job.
- The mower will not start.
- When the mower is jump-started, the battery does not charge.

Try rewriting Bart's memo. Compare your version to this one.

> Bob,
>
> The riding lawn mower we put a rebuilt alternator into three weeks ago isn't starting. When we jump-start it, the battery doesn't charge. I think the alternator is broken again. We need this fixed right away if we're going to be ready for the convention next week. Would you please see that the mower gets fixed? Thank you.
>
> Bart

Answers

Keep in mind that there are many ways to correct a fragment. In some answers, only one is printed. In the answers to sentences 7 and 10, the subjects have been bolded and the verbs underlined.

1. The next train will be arriving five minutes from now.
   Five minutes from now, the next train will be arriving.
2. Not liking it one bit, Jane ate the casserole.
   Jane ate the casserole, not liking it one bit.
3. They used a fog machine from an Army surplus store to create the effect of smoke.
4. Send your news on letterhead stationery to represent your company.
5. The judge ran out of patience not long before the last witness had testified.
   Not long before the last witness had testified, the judge ran out of patience.
6. Wishing he were almost anywhere else, Steve moaned and hung his head.
7. **Sentence.** In the end, **it** <u>made</u> no difference at all.
8. The Kern family thought that camping outside would be fun.
9. Before the part stops working completely, we should order a replacement.
10. **Sentence.** The unidentified **man** <u>looked</u> like a reporter.

CHAPTER 4 GRAMMAR IQ QUIZ

Add punctuation marks wherever needed in the following sentences. You may also need to capitalize a word in some of the sentences. Answers follow the quiz.

1. Mavis delivered the package it arrived a day ahead of schedule.
2. Scott was running late the traffic was unusually heavy.
3. The electricians finished on time however they overspent their budget.
4. You'll need to reorganize these files otherwise we'll never be able to find anything.
5. Beverly needed some advice she was at the end of her rope.

Answers

1. Mavis delivered the package. It arrived a day ahead of schedule.

   or

   Mavis delivered the package; it arrived a day ahead of schedule.
2. Scott was running late. The traffic was unusually heavy.

   or

   Scott was running late; the traffic was unusually heavy.
3. The electricians finished on time; however, they overspent their budget.

   or

   The electricians finished on time. However, they overspent their budget.
4. You'll need to reorganize these files; otherwise, we'll never be able to find anything.

   or

   You'll need to reorganize these files. Otherwise, we'll never be able to find anything.
5. Beverly needed some advice. She was at the end of her rope.

   or

   Beverly needed some advice; she was at the end of her rope.

CHAPTER

PUTTING A STOP TO GOING ON AND ON

This chapter explains how to spot two problems that can keep people from understanding what you write: run-on sentences and comma splices. This chapter shows you how to correct and avoid both of these problems.

Grammar concepts to know:

- **run-on sentence**—independent clauses that run together without punctuation
- **comma splice**—only a comma separates two independent clauses (a semicolon or a comma followed by a conjunction are required)
- **conjunctive adverb**—an adverb, such as *however* or *therefore*, that expresses a relationship between clauses

Have you heard any of the radio or TV advertisements that use speed speakers, those people who can utter four or five sentences in five seconds? What they say is difficult for a listener to understand because there is no pause in the sound. The same thing can happen in writing. Read the memo on the following page. Although you can probably understand what it says, doing so will not be easy. In fact, you may need to read the memo several times to figure out its meaning.

To: Arlis Schaffer
From: Gerald Lentz
Re: New floor buffer
Date: March 5, 2006

The buffer we got last week from Holton Supply has a few problems it doesn't always start when you flip the switch and it seems a little hesitant like it loses power every once in a while when I'm running it also the pads that came with it don't fit exactly right they are about an inch too small when the machine runs the outside part of it is not covered and often scratches the floor that's not good because it takes me forever to work out the scratches that the machine is supposed to avoid making instead of saving me time this machine is costing me more time. We need someone to look at the switch and we need to order the right size pads and it wouldn't hurt to see if they can find anything else wrong with this machine I just don't trust it.

This memo is hard to understand because some of the sentences "run on" without a break. We call these run-on sentences. This chapter shows you how to avoid and correct run-on sentences when you write.

RUN-ON SENTENCES

As you know, an independent clause is a group of words that could be a complete sentence on its own. In a **run-on sentence**, independent clauses are run together as one sentence without being separated by any punctuation (a period, semicolon, or comma).

The best way to avoid run-on sentences is to practice writing simple sentences, each explaining one thought. When you finish explaining one thought, end the sentence. Your sentences will be very short, but they will also be easy to understand.

Sanjay packed the suitcase.
Oded loaded the car.
Sandra drove through the storm.
Jake unloaded the luggage.

Quite often, more than one idea must be presented in a sentence. As discussed in Chapter 2, this kind of sentence, which is called a compound sentence, is made up of two or more independent clauses. When written correctly, the clauses are separated by conjunctions and/or punctuation. The sentences that follow contain more than one independent clause, but the clauses have been run together without words or punctuation. This makes them run-on sentences.

Lissie moved to the suburbs she still kept in touch with her friends in the city.
My paycheck this week is more than I thought it would be now I can buy the computer I've been wanting.
I started a new exercise regime a month ago I've lost three and a half pounds already.

All three of these examples can be corrected quite easily in one of four ways:

1. By adding a period and a capital letter, making two simple sentences.
Lissie moved to the suburbs. She still kept in touch with her friends in the city.
My paycheck this week is more than I thought it would be. Now I can buy the computer I've been wanting.
I started a new exercise regime a month ago. I've lost three and a half pounds already.

2. By adding a comma and a conjunction (*and, but, or, for, nor, yet, so*).
Lissie moved to the suburbs, but she still kept in touch with her friends in the city.
My paycheck this week is more than I thought it would be, so now I can buy the computer I've been wanting.
I started a new exercise regime a month ago, and I've lost three and a half pounds already.

3. By adding a semicolon.
Lissie moved to the suburbs; she still kept in touch with her friends in the city.
My paycheck this week is more than I thought it would be; now I can buy the computer I've been wanting.
I started a new exercise regime a month ago; I've lost three and a half pounds already.

4. By turning one of the two independent clauses into a dependent clause. To do this, you need to add a subordinating conjunction where it best fits in the sentence and reword the sentence, if necessary. Refer to the list of subordinating conjunctions from the last chapter to refresh your memory.

   Although she moved to the suburbs, Lissie still kept in touch with her friends in the city.
   Lissie still kept in touch with her friends in the city **although** she moved to the suburbs.

   Since my paycheck this week is more than I thought it would be, now I can buy the computer I've been wanting.
   Now I can buy the computer I've been wanting **since** my paycheck this week is more than I thought it would be.

   Because I started a new exercise regime a month ago, I've lost three and a half pounds already.
   I've lost three and a half pounds already **because** I started a new exercise regime a month ago.

In these examples, all three sentences have been rewritten in two ways: by putting the dependent clause at the beginning of the sentence and by putting it at the end. Notice how if the dependent clause comes first, it is set off by a comma. No comma is needed if the dependent clause follows the independent clause.

Practice

Look at each of the following run-on sentences. Correct them so they are no longer run-on. Check your work with the answers at the end of the chapter.

1. The personnel director gave us bonus checks the president shook our hands.
2. Evelyn signed the work order she gave it to the secretary.
3. Sam listens to music when he works it relaxes him.
4. Barry took the short cut he ended up lost.
5. My sweatshirt was ruined I spilled grape juice on it.

COMMA SPLICES

Another kind of problem sentence, called a **comma splice**, is unclear for the reader because only a comma is used to separate two independent clauses.

Mr. Klein is bald, his wife has long frizzy hair.
Jacob did the raking, Matthew did the mowing.
Weldon bought the groceries, Nancy cooked dinner.

Comma splices can be fixed in the same ways that run-on sentences can.

1. Separate independent clauses with a comma and a conjunction (*and, but, so, or, for, nor, yet*).

 Mr. Klein is bald, but his wife has long frizzy hair.
 Jacob did the raking, and Matthew did the mowing.
 Weldon bought the groceries, so Nancy cooked dinner.

2. Separate independent clauses with a semicolon.

 Mr. Klein is bald; his wife has long frizzy hair.
 Jacob did the raking; Matthew did the mowing.
 Weldon bought the groceries; Nancy cooked dinner.

3. Separate the two clauses into two sentences by replacing the comma with a period and by adding a capital letter.

 Mr. Klein is bald. His wife has long frizzy hair.
 Jacob did the raking. Matthew did the mowing.
 Weldon bought the groceries. Nancy cooked dinner.

4. Turn one of the clauses into a dependent clause by adding a subordinating conjunction, if it makes sense to do so.

 While Mr. Klein is bald, his wife has long frizzy hair.
 Because Jacob did the raking, Matthew did the mowing.
 After Weldon bought the groceries, Nancy cooked dinner.

Practice

Read the sentences with comma splices that follow. Correct them so that each is a correctly written sentence. Check your work with the answers at the end of the chapter.

6. Henry lives across the street, he has been there for twenty-five years.
7. Mary heads the search committee, John is the recorder.
8. Sid gave demonstrations all summer long, he returned in the fall.
9. Mary posted the work schedule, Peter requested a change.
10. Kent brought the problem to our attention, we fixed it immediately.

CONJUNCTIVE ADVERBS

Some run-on sentences and commas splices are created by using words such as *however, therefore,* and *then* as though they were conjunctions.

> I wanted a new sports car however my bank account wouldn't support one.
>
> My sister Dorothy thought she was cheated, therefore, she wanted her money back.
>
> We stopped for lunch then we got back to work.

Unlike conjunctions, which simply join words together, words such as *however, therefore,* and *then* are a special kind of adverb that expresses a relationship between clauses. This kind of adverb, called a **conjunctive adverb**, cannot join two independent clauses the way a conjunction does.

To correct this kind of comma splice or run-on, make two sentences, or put a semicolon between the two main clauses and set the adverb off from the rest of the clause with a comma. Note that you can move the adverb around within its clause without changing the meaning—which is how you can tell the difference between a conjunctive adverb and a subordinate conjunction. You can move *however* around in its clause, but you can't move *because* around in its clause.

> I wanted a new sports car. However, my bank account wouldn't support one.
>
> I wanted a new sports car; however, my bank account wouldn't support one.
>
> I wanted a new sports car; my bank account, however, wouldn't support one.

My sister Dorothy thought she was cheated. She therefore wanted her money back.
My sister Dorothy thought she was cheated; therefore, she wanted her money back.
My sister Dorothy thought she was cheated; she therefore wanted her money back

We stopped for lunch. Then we got back to work.
We stopped for lunch; then we got back to work.
We stopped for lunch. We then got back to work.

Practice

Use what you have learned about commas and semicolons to correct the following sentences. Check your work with the answers at the end of the chapter.

11. These microscope cases are falling apart the lenses of these microscopes however are very durable.
12. Maribeth's coat was in the cloakroom however she had left an hour ago.
13. A drug test is not required for this job the central office will need your fingerprints however.

Remember the memo from the beginning of the chapter? Go back to it and correct the run-on sentences. Compare your version with the one printed here.

To: Arlis Schaffer
From: Gerald Lentz
Re: New floor buffer
Date: March 5, 1997

The buffer we got last week from Holton Supply has a few problems. It doesn't always start up when you flip the switch, and it seems a little hesitant. It loses power every once in a while when I'm running it. Also, the pads that came with it don't fit exactly right. They are about an inch too small. When the machine runs, the outside part of it is not covered, so it often scratches the floor. That's not good because it takes me forever to work out the scratches that the machine is supposed to avoid making. Instead of saving me time, this machine is costing me more time. We need someone to look at the switch, and we need to order the right size pads. It wouldn't hurt to see if they can find anything else wrong with this machine. I just don't trust it.

REVIEW

Here is an opportunity to practice what you have learned about complete sentences, sentence fragments, run-ons, and comma splices. In each of the following numbered items, decide whether the group of words is a correctly written sentence or sentences. If it is not, rewrite it to make it correct. Check your version with the ones given at the end of the chapter.

14. Mr. France introduced me to the speaker. A neighbor of his.
15. Last night my supervisor called. To ask me if I could stay an extra three hours today.
16. I like the new batch of chemicals, they keep mildew from forming on wet surfaces.
17. I looked in my mailbox. Hoping to find my paycheck.
18. I saw it. The key I had lost.
19. After I had read the entire manual.
20. Jeremy filled the order, it arrived at the warehouse around noon.
21. Ilya locked the doors we left the building.
22. Our surveillance system has cut down on shoplifting.
23. Lying on the floor next to the coffee table.

Answers

1. The personnel director gave us bonus checks. The president shook our hands.
The personnel director gave us bonus checks, and the president shook our hands.
The personnel director gave us bonus checks while the president shook our hands.

2. Evelyn signed the work order. She gave it to the secretary.
Evelyn signed the work order, and she gave it to the secretary.
Evelyn signed the work order before she gave it to the secretary.

3. Sam listens to music when he works. It relaxes him.
Sam listens to music when he works, and it relaxes him.
Sam listens to music when he works because it relaxes him.

4. Barry took the short cut. He ended up lost.
Barry took the short cut, and he ended up lost.
Because Barry took the short cut, he ended up lost.

5. My sweatshirt was ruined. I spilled grape juice on it.
I spilled grape juice on my sweatshirt, and it was ruined.
My sweatshirt was ruined because I spilled grape juice on it.

6. Henry lives across the street; he has been there for twenty-five years.
Henry lives across the street, and he has been there for twenty-five years.
Henry lives across the street. He has been there for twenty-five years.
(This is an example of a situation where adding a subordinating conjunction would not make sense.)

7. Mary heads the search committee; John is the recorder.
Mary heads the search committee, and John is the recorder.
Mary heads the search committee. John is the recorder.
While Mary heads the search committee, John is the recorder.

8. Sid gave demonstrations all summer long; he returned in the fall.
Sid gave demonstrations all summer long, and he returned in the fall.
Sid gave demonstrations all summer long. He returned in the summer.
After Sid gave demonstrations all summer long, he returned in the summer.

9. Mary posted the work schedule; Peter requested a change.
Mary posted the work schedule, and Peter requested a change.
Mary posted the work schedule. Peter requested a change.
After Mary posted the work schedule, Peter requested a change.

10. Kent brought the problem to our attention; we fixed it immediately.
Kent brought the problem to our attention, and we fixed it immediately.
Kent brought the problem to our attention. We fixed it immediately.
When Kent brought the problem to our attention, we fixed it immediately.

11. These microscope cases are falling apart; the lenses of these microscopes, however, are very durable.

12. Maribeth's coat was in the cloakroom; however, she had left an hour ago.

13. A drug test is not required for this job; the central office will need your fingerprints, however.

14. Mr. France introduced me to the speaker, a neighbor of his.

15. Last night my supervisor called to ask me if I could stay an extra three hours today.

16. I like the new batch of chemicals; they keep mildew from forming on wet surfaces.
I like the new batch of chemicals because they keep mildew from forming on wet surfaces.

17. I looked in my mailbox, hoping to find my paycheck.

18. I saw it, the key I had lost.

19. After I had read the entire manual, I understood how to operate the equipment.

20. Jeremy filled the order. It arrived at the warehouse around noon.
Jeremy filled the order when it arrived at the warehouse around noon.

21. Ilya locked the doors. We left the building.
Ilya locked the doors, and we left the building.
Ilya locked the doors after we left the building.

22. Sentence

23. We found the lost catalog lying on the floor next to the coffee table.

CHAPTER 5 GRAMMAR IQ QUIZ

Place an end mark (period, question mark, exclamation point) after each of the following sentences. Add capital letters wherever they are needed. Answers follow the quiz.

1. henry drives a jeep cherokee and works at nelson manufacturing
2. when did president bush climb aboard air force one and fly to washington, dc
3. next year the math course i will be taking is called industrial math applications
4. did you know that my uncle harry sold his car to aunt edna
5. how nice of mr. bosselman to accommodate our wishes to move to 345 ingersoll avenue

Answers

1. Henry drives a Jeep Cherokee and works at Nelson Manufacturing.
2. When did President Bush climb aboard Air Force One and fly to Washington, D.C.?
3. Next year, the math course I will be taking is called Industrial Math Applications.
4. Did you know that my uncle Harry sold his car to Aunt Edna?
5. How nice of Mr. Bosselman to accommodate our wishes to move to 345 Ingersoll Avenue!

CHAPTER

GOOD BEGINNINGS, GOOD ENDINGS

Now that you know what a sentence is, it's a good idea to review how to begin and end one. This chapter shows you how to use capital letters—and not only those at the beginnings of sentences—as well as periods, question marks, and exclamation points.

Grammar concepts to know:
- **proper noun**—the name of a particular person, place, or thing
- **proper adjective**—an adjective (a word that describes) derived from a proper noun

Capital letters are necessary beginnings—not only for sentences, but also for all kinds of words. Periods are sometimes necessary endings, not only for most sentences, but also for abbreviations and other uses. Question marks and exclamation points, too, are necessary in some sentences, and can provide a little spice to your writing. This chapter helps you master capitalization and punctuation.

Read this memo from Mike:

> I need a New router and a Band saw. Wards has them on sale this week. A skil saw would be nice sometimes one isn't enough since there are three of us who use it. Black and decker is also okay? If you want, I can pick them up at the store for you.
>
> Mike

What exactly does Mike want? The first sentence makes it clear that he wants a router and a saw. The rest of the memo leads to nothing but questions: Does he want a band saw made by Skil, or a circular saw (sometimes called a skill saw) by Band? This confusion comes up because Mike hasn't punctuated his memo properly or put capital letters where they belong.

CAPITAL LETTERS

General Capitalization Rules

Here are some rules for capitalization.

- Capitalize the first word of a sentence. If the first word is a number, write it as a word.

  This is my favorite dish.
  Four people showed up to volunteer.

- Capitalize the pronoun *I* or any contraction made using *I (I'm, I'd, I've, I'll).*

  The professor told me that **I** needed to take a prerequisite before taking his class.
  She thought that **I'd** decide to move to California.
  I know **I'll** be ready for this exam.

- Capitalize proper nouns, but not common nouns.

  A proper noun refers to a specific person, place, or thing. A common noun refers to a general class of people, places, or things. For example, *microwave* is a common noun. It is the general name for a kitchen appliance. However, Sharp is a proper noun because it names a specific brand of microwave. Proper nouns are capitalized; common nouns are not.

Proper Nouns	**Common Nouns**
Tom	uncle
Georgia	state
Charleston Memorial	hospital
Labrador Retriever	dog
Dell	computer

- Capitalize the first word of a quotation.

  "When will you be finished?"
  My new neighbor said "Good morning," as I approached the door.
  "Good morning!" I answered, somewhat surprised. "You must be Sylvia."

- Do *not* capitalize the first word of a partial quotation.

  He called her "the best problem solver alive."
  "The new edition," Ari explained, "will be available in two months."

Practice

Check your knowledge of these rules with the following sentences. Circle the letters that should be capitalized in each sentence. Make a diagonal mark through the letters that are capitalized, but should not be. Check your work with the correct versions of sentences at the end of the chapter. The changes are bolded for you.

1. the instructions were clear. after a careful reading, i could understand them completely.
2. "what do you think you're doing?" my Uncle jack asked.
3. "i'm putting together this gas grill," i answered.
4. the newspaper said our new owner was "An industrial visionary."
5. my new Car is a ford mustang.

Proper Nouns

All proper nouns—words that name a specific person, place, or thing—must be capitalized. Remembering which nouns are proper can be difficult. The table that follows includes the most common categories of proper nouns.

Category of Proper Nouns	Example
days of the week	Sunday, Tuesday
months	March, April
holidays	Easter, Passover
historical events, periods, documents	Revolutionary War (event) Middle Ages (period) U.S. Constitution (document)
special events, calendar events	Chili Cook-Off Mother's Day Memorial Day
names of people and places	Steven Jones, Kennedy Center, Empire State Building
names of structures, buildings	Lincoln Memorial, Travelers Building
names of trains, ships, aircraft, other	Queen Elizabeth, Discovery, Northern
modes of transportation	Pacific, Vanguard Airlines
names of products	Dial soap, Jeep Cherokee
names of officials	Senator Kennedy, President Bush
works of art and literature	Tobacco Road (book) "Harlem" (poem)
ethnic groups, races, languages, nationalities	Italian American, Asian, German, Spanish
cities, states, and governmental units	Sioux City, Iowa; Anchorage, Alaska; Republic of China
streets, highways, and roads	Locust Avenue, Interstate 80, Havelin Boulevard
landmarks and geographical locations	Rocky Mountains, International Date Line
public areas and bodies of water	Chippewa Forest, Raccoon River
institutions, organizations, and businesses	Luther College, Rotary Club, Bellwether Ford

Practice

Using these rules, circle the letters that should be capitalized in each of the following sentences. Make a diagonal mark through any letters that are capitalized, but should not be. Check your work with the corrected versions of the sentences at the end of the chapter. The changes are in bold for you in the answers.

6. shakespeare was the most prolific author of the renaissance.
7. the nelsons spent thanksgiving Day with Relatives.
8. andy began work on thursday, april 3.
9. my Friend jon has two Nephews who fought in iraq
10. Additional Security guards will be hired for the white stripes concert.
11. The convention group caught the amtrak in omaha.
12. Ling applied for admission to the university of Iowa.
13. In canada, some citizens speak french, and others speak english.
14. We followed the colorado river to the border of arizona.
15. Ammar works for apex construction company.

Proper Adjectives

An **adjective** is a word that describes or tells us more about a person, place, or thing. A proper adjective is derived from a proper noun. Many proper adjectives refer to a nationality. Most proper adjectives should be capitalized, such as *English muffin, Polish sausage,* and *French customs.*

Practice

Circle the letters that should be capitalized in the following sentences. Check your work with the corrected versions of the sentences at the end of the chapter. The changes are bolded for you.

16. Amasu prefers italian dressing on her salad.
17. When I win the lottery, I intend to buy a polynesian island.
18. We were delayed at the canadian border.

When Not to Capitalize

- Avoid unnecessarily capitalizing compass directions. However, direction words that refer to a specific area of the country should be capitalized. Direction words are not capitalized unless they specifically refer to a part of the country.

  We headed east to avoid the storm.
  The computer industry flourished in the West.

- Avoid unnecessarily capitalizing words that refer to family members. Capitalize them only if they are used as names.

  Although Aunt Matilda has arrived, my other aunts are late.
  After my mother lectured me, Father grounded me.

Look closely at the second example. If a word such as *my, our, your, his, her,* or *their* comes before the word that refers to a family member, it is not capitalized. The word *mother* is not capitalized because the word *my* comes before it. However, no such word comes before *Father.* In fact, *Father* is used in place of the man's name, making it a proper name. That is why it is capitalized.

- Avoid unnecessarily capitalizing the seasons of the year or parts of the academic year.

  The university offers Basic Computing 405 in the spring semester.
  Marge plants her perennials in the early fall.

- Avoid unnecessarily capitalizing school subjects. They should be capitalized only if they are part of the name of a specific course.

  I try to avoid science courses because I'm squeamish.
  Nyrupama is taking Biology II next semester.

- Avoid unnecessarily capitalizing words modified by proper adjectives.

  Polish sausage, not Polish Sausage
  Italian restaurant, not Italian Restaurant

Practice

Using these rules, circle the letters that should be capitalized in each of the following sentences. Make a diagonal mark through any letters that are capitalized but should not be. Check your work with the corrected versions of the sentences at the end of the chapter. The changes are bolded for you.

19. The great plains are located in the midwest.
20. Cynthia turned West at the stop sign.
21. If my Cousin Kathy comes to the picnic, I know aunt Jan won't.
22. Jacob is an outstanding History student.
23. We went to a sri lankan Restaurant in minneapolis.

END PUNCTUATION

When to Use Question Marks

Use a question mark after a word or a group of words that asks a question.

Why?
Really?
Where did you get your hair cut?
What time does he get home?

Sentences that begin with these words are usually questions:

who	*where*
what	*why*
when	*how*

When to Use Periods

- Use a period at the end of a sentence that makes a statement.

  Many jobs require a working knowledge of computers.
  Thomas Jefferson is the most famous American slave owner.
  The tour bus leaves right after breakfast in the morning.

- Use a period at the end of sentence that makes a request, gives an instruction, or states a command.

  Take this to the mailbox before you leave.
  Open the cover, remove item B, and close the box.
  Check the message board before you go home.

- Use a period—not a question mark—at the end of a sentence that asks an indirect question.

  My boss asked if I had seen her coat. (indirect question)
  Have you seen my coat? (direct question)

  Hayden wanted to know how we knew what to do. (indirect question)
  How did you know what to do? (direct question)

Rachel asked if I would help her. (indirect question)
Will you help me? (direct question)

Practice

Place a period or a question mark at the end of each of these sentences. Check your work with the corrected versions of the sentences at the end of the chapter. The changes are bolded for you.

24. Cyril asked me to find the new order that arrived today
25. Do you think we'll be finished by the end of the day
26. Today is colder than yesterday
27. When do you plan to order the supplies we need
28. Leave the packages on the counter by the window

Other Uses for Periods

- Use a period (also called a *decimal point*) before a decimal.

  A gallon equals 3.875 liters.
  Only 5.6% of our employees chose vision care.

- Use a period between dollars and cents.

  The new paneling costs $45.95 a sheet.
  Do you have $4.50 that I can borrow?

- Use a period after an initial in a personal name.

  The patient in room 202 is Ron P. Martel.
  The book was written by J.R.R. Tolkien.
  A.J. Foyt races cars.

- Use a period after an abbreviation.

  The plane leaves at 3:17 on Jan. 1.
  Smith Bros. is hiring subcontractors for this job.
  The apt. complex at the corner of Woodland Ave. and 1st St. belongs to me.

When Not to Use Periods

- If an abbreviation comes at the end of a sentence, only one period is needed.

We delivered the desk to Koch & Co.
This trailer was machined at Dee Zee Inc.
The box is 3 in. by 5 in.

- If an abbreviation has become a commonly used name for something, no period is needed.

gym (gymnasium)
exam (examination)
auto (automobile)

- If an abbreviation has become an acronym, or a name widely recognized by its initials (TV, WHO, FBI, NATO, NASA), no period is needed.

Velma is scheduled for an MRI at 3:00 this afternoon.
The Smiths mailed their tax forms to the IRS.
My niece works for the CIA.

Practice

Use what you know about periods to correct these sentences. Check your sentences with the corrected sentences at the end of the chapter. The changes are bolded for you.

29. The plane left Omaha, Neb, and arrived at Tampa Bay, Fl, at 2:23
30. Mr Drish and Dr P M Staplin left for the convention this morning
31. The patients' rooms measured 14 ft by 17 ft
32. I sold my used CD for $3 99
33. Go ahead Explain what you mean

When to Use Exclamation Points

- Use an exclamation point after an outcry or sentence that expresses strong feeling.

You're kidding!
Oh, no!
That's unbelievable!
Be careful!

Warning! Exclamation points are a little bit like salt on food. Be careful not to overdo them.

- Use an exclamation point after an exclamation that begins with a question word (*who, what, when, where, why, how*) but doesn't ask a question.

  How forgetful I am!
  What a lot of trouble for such a small result!

Practice

Use what you know about questions marks, periods, and exclamation points to correct these sentences. Check your work with the corrected versions of the sentences at the end of the chapter. The changes are bolded for you.

34. Help! I can't breathe?
35. I got my income tax forms in the mail today!
36. Will you check this order for me.
37. Those plumbers? Do you know what they did!
38. I'm amazed at how quickly she moved?

REVIEW

Remember the memo from Mike at the beginning of the chapter? He rewrote it using proper capitalization and endmarks. Now his supervisor knows exactly what he wants.

> I need a new router and a band saw. Sometimes, one saw isn't enough since there are three of us who use it. A Skil saw would be nice. Black and Decker is also okay. Wards has them on sale this week. If you want, I can pick them up at the store for you.
>
> Mike

Answers

1. The instructions were clear. **A**fter a careful reading, **I** could understand them completely.
2. "**W**hat do you think you're doing?" my **u**ncle **J**ack asked.
3. "**I**'m putting together this gas grill," **I** answered.
4. The newspaper said our new owner was "**a**n industrial visionary."

5. My new car is a Ford Mustang.
6. Shakespeare was the most prolific author of the Renaissance.
7. The Nelsons spent Thanksgiving Day with relatives.
8. Andy began work on Thursday, April 3.
9. My friend Jon has two nephews who fought in Iraq.
10. Additional security guards will be hired for the White Stripes concert.
11. The convention group caught the Amtrak in Omaha.
12. Ling applied for admission to the University of Iowa.
13. In Canada, some citizens speak French, and others speak English.
14. We followed the Colorado River to the border of Arizona.
15. Ammar works for Apex Construction Company.
16. Amasu prefers Italian dressing on her salad.
17. When I win the lottery, I intend to buy a Polynesian island.
18. We were delayed at the Canadian border.
19. The Great Plains are located in the Midwest.
20. Cynthia turned west at the stop sign.
21. If my cousin Kathy comes to the picnic, I know Aunt Jan won't.
22. Jacob is an outstanding history student.
23. We went to a Sri Lankan restaurant in Minneapolis.
24. Cyril asked me to find the new order that arrived today.
25. Do you think we'll be finished by the end of the day?
26. Today is colder than yesterday.
27. When do you plan to order the supplies we need?
28. Leave the packages on the counter by the window.
29. The plane left Omaha, Neb., and arrived at Tampa Bay, Fl., at 2:23.
30. Mr. Drish and Dr. P. M. Staplin left for the convention this morning.
31. The patients' rooms measured 14 ft. by 17 ft.
32. I sold my used CD for $3.99.
33. Go ahead. Explain what you mean.
34. Help! I can't breathe!
35. I got my income tax forms in the mail today.
36. Will you check this order for me?
37. Those plumbers! Do you know what they did?
38. I'm amazed at how quickly she moved!

CHAPTER 6 GRAMMAR IQ QUIZ

Add commas where they are needed in the following sentences. Answers and explanations follow the quiz.

1. Discouraged Sari decided to wait until next year to retake the exam.
2. Enjoying himself Julio decided to stay at the party.
3. As long as she is president of the committee your job is safe.
4. My dessert crème Brule was not as good as when I make it at home.
5. The dog that is blind in one eye is the one I want to adopt.
6. Ahmed who studied international relations in college wants to go into politics.

Answers

1. Discouraged, Sari decided to wait until next year to retake the exam. (sets off an introductory word)
2. Enjoying himself, Julio decided to stay at the party. (sets off an introductory phrase)
3. As long as she is president of the committee, your job is safe. (sets off an introductory clause)
4. My dessert, crème Brule, was not as good as when I make it at home. (sets off a nonessential explaining phrase)
5. The dog that is blind in one eye is the one I want to adopt. (No comma needed—the clause is essential to the meaning of the sentence.)
6. Ahmed, who studied international relations in college, wants to go into politics. (sets off a nonessential clause)

CHAPTER

COMMA SENSE

Commas are like road signs. They give us direction, tell us where to pause, and make information clear to us. This chapter explains some of the ways to use commas in sentences.

Grammar concepts to know:

- **essential clause**—a dependent clause necessary to the basic meaning of a sentence; removing the clause would alter the meaning of the sentence
- **nonessential clause**—a dependent clause that is not necessary to the basic meaning of a sentence; removing it would not cause the meaning of the sentence to change

This chapter shows how to use commas to separate different parts of sentences. (As you go through this chapter, remember what you have already learned about sentences, fragments, run-ons, and comma splices.) You will learn how to use commas to set off introductory sentence parts, explaining phrases, and nonessential clauses.

SETTING OFF INTRODUCTORY SENTENCE PARTS

Use a comma to set off introductory words, phrases, and clauses from the main part of a sentence. A comma keeps the reader from accidentally attaching the introductory portion to the main part of the sentence, then having to go back and reread the sentence. In other words, commas following introductory elements will save the reader time and reduce the chances of misinterpreting what is written. Read the examples that follow to see how introductory words, phrases, and clauses are set off with commas.

- **Words**

    Relieved, I gathered my things and left for the day.
    Surprised, I backed into a table.
    Amazed, the doctor revised his patient's medication.

- **Phrases**

    Hoping for the best, we checked our findings.
    Badly injured in the accident, Steve was hospitalized for three months.
    Fooled by the pitch, the batter missed the ball.

- **Clauses**

    When he called me, I was in the middle of cooking dinner.
    Although it was hot outside, I still cooked a barbecue.
    Since we arrived late, we decided to skip dinner.

Introductory clauses are dependent clauses because they cannot stand alone. In the clause examples above, the dependent clause is followed by a comma because it is introducing the rest of the sentence. If the two parts of each of these sentences were reversed, the sentence would still make sense. However, if you reverse the sentence parts, placing the dependent clause at the end, you do *not* need a comma.

I was in the middle of cooking dinner when he called me.
I still cooked a barbecue although it was hot outside.
We decided to skip dinner since we arrived late.

Practice

Use what you know about commas to correct these sentences. Check your work with the corrected versions at the end of the chapter. The changes are bolded for you.

1. Concerned about his future Brad went back to school.
2. Soaking in the stainless-steel sink his shirt looked doomed.
3. I gathered all the supplies, before I started work this morning.
4. By repairing the equipment ourselves we saved several days.
5. Ecstatic the coach hugged the referee.
6. I will remember how to assemble this vacuum, as long as I have the directions.
7. As far as I know the guests in that room checked out an hour ago.
8. Outside the yard was covered with flowers.
9. After running the horses returned to the barn.
10. During the night time drags on and on.
11. As he watched the clock slowly ticked away the seconds.

SETTING OFF EXPLAINING PHRASES

An **explaining phrase** is a word or group of words that immediately follows a noun or pronoun. The phrase makes the noun or pronoun clearer or more definite by explaining or identifying it. (An explaining phrase is also called an *appositive.*) If the explaining phrase is not essential to the meaning of the sentence, it is set off by commas, as in the following examples. Look at these examples. The explaining phrases have been bolded.

> Mindy Wilcox ordered dinner, **a thick filet with steamed vegetables**.
> Melanie Hicklin, **our company nurse**, will give flu shots tomorrow.
> The keynote speaker is Mary Swenson, **director of the Animal Rescue League**.

Sometimes, an identifying proper noun will precede or follow a common noun. If the proper noun is necessary to identify the person, place, or thing, it is not set off by commas. However, if the person can be identified without the proper noun, then the proper noun is surrounded by commas.

> My brother, **David,** farms and ranches in South Dakota.
> The shock rocker **Marilyn Manson** performed at the Civic Center.
> The vice-president, **Dick Cheney,** visited the flood site.

Whenever information not essential to the meaning of a sentence is added, that information is set off by commas. Look closely at the first example. The presence of commas tells us that the writer has only one brother. *David* is set off by commas because *brother* is enough information to identify the subject. The name David simply adds additional information. However, in the second example, we know that more than one shock rocker exists since the name Marilyn Manson is not set off by commas.

Practice

Use what you have learned to add commas to the following sentences. Check your work with the answers at the end of the chapter. The changes are bolded for you.

12. Air quality a major urban problem has steadily improved over the last few years.
13. Walter the featured artist delivered a stunning presentation.
14. Sharon spends Friday evenings at the movies an event she looks forward to all week.
15. Ms. Mason the route manager always leaves the papers at the corner.
16. The two sisters Kim and Jessica looked nothing alike.

ESSENTIAL CLAUSES

At the beginning of this chapter, you learned that an introductory dependent clause is followed by a comma, but when the same clause is moved to the end of the sentence, no comma is needed. In some sentences, a dependent clause cannot be omitted without changing the basic meaning of the sentence. Omitting it alters the meaning of the sentence or makes it untrue. Such a clause is an **essential clause** (also known as a *restrictive clause*) and it is also not set off by commas. You can see how this works in the following sentences.

> All drivers **who have had a drunk driving conviction** should have their licenses revoked.
> All drivers should have their licenses revoked.

The bolded clause is essential because the meaning of the sentence is changed if the clause is removed from the sentence. The lack of commas shows that the clause is essential.

NONESSENTIAL CLAUSES

A **nonessential** clause adds information that is not essential to the basic meaning of the sentence. If a nonessential clause is removed, the basic meaning of the sentence is not changed. Just like nonessential phrases, nonessential clauses (also known as *nonrestrictive clauses*) are set off by commas. See how this works in the following examples.

> Matt's mother, **who has trouble with directions**, had to ask for help.
> Matt's mother had to ask for help.

The bolded clause is nonessential because if it is removed from the sentence, the basic meaning of the sentence does not change. To show that it is nonessential, it is set off by commas. Nonessential clauses usually begin with one of these words: *who, whom, whose, which,* or *that.*

Practice

Each of the following sentences contains a dependent clause, which is bolded for you. If the clause is essential, do not add commas. If it is nonessential, set it off with commas. Check your work with the answers at the end of the chapter.

17. Mr. Lindgren is not a man **who likes to be fooled**.
18. Nicole lives on Briarwood Drive **which is south of the freeway**.
19. The cattle **that were vaccinated** are immune to mad cow disease.
20. Children **who are born on February 29** start school before they are two.
21. The mall restaurant offers free beverages to anyone **who orders a dinner**.
22. Josh **who is very outgoing** has become one of my best friends.

REVIEW

It's time for a real challenge. This next exercise contains no commas, endmarks, or capital letters. Use what you have learned so far to add capital letters, endmarks, and commas to make sense of the paragraph. Check your work with the corrected version at the end of the chapter.

> because mary and velma were morning people they met for breakfast every day before work they met at village inn on the corner of university ave and swanson blvd usually they had a light breakfast of bagels with cream cheese and coffee whenever one of them had something to celebrate they would order english muffins and omelettes something neither of them liked to make themselves how they enjoyed those mornings

they had a host of special rules regarding these special omelettes what were those rules if one of them was celebrating a birthday they ordered omelettes with something red such as tomatoes or red peppers mary's birthday was feb 22 velma's was oct 12 if one of them had received a raise they ordered omelettes with green peppers or green onions only once when velma won the lottery did they order omelettes with cheese and bacon

Answers

1. Concerned about his future, Brad went back to school.
2. Soaking in the stainless-steel sink, his shirt looked doomed.
3. I gathered all the supplies before I started work this morning.
4. By repairing the equipment ourselves, we saved several days.
5. Ecstatic, the coach hugged the referee.
6. I will remember how to assemble this vacuum as long as I have directions.
7. As far as I know, the guests in that room checked out an hour ago.
8. Outside, the yard was covered with flowers.
9. After running, the horses returned to the barn.
10. During the night, time drags on and on.
11. As he watched, the clock slowly ticked away the seconds.
12. Air quality, a major urban problem, has steadily improved over the last few years.
13. Walter, the featured artist, delivered a stunning presentation.
14. Sharon spends Friday evenings at the movies, an event she looks forward to all week.
15. Ms. Mason, the route manager, always leaves the papers at the corner.
16. The two sisters, Kim and Jessica, looked nothing alike.
17. Essential clause. No commas needed.
18. Nicole lives on Briarwood Drive, which is south of the freeway.
19. Essential clause. No commas needed.
20. Essential clause. No commas needed.
21. Essential clause. No commas needed.
22. Josh, who is very outgoing, has become one of my best friends.

REVIEW

Because Mary and Velma were morning people, they met for breakfast every day before work. They met at Village Inn on the corner of University Ave. and Swanson Blvd. Usually, they had a light breakfast of bagels with cream cheese and coffee. Whenever one of them had something to celebrate, they would order English muffins and omelettes, something neither of them liked to make themselves. How they enjoyed those mornings!

They had a host of special rules regarding these special omelettes. What were those rules? If one of them was celebrating a birthday, they ordered omelettes with something red, such as tomatoes or red peppers. Mary's birthday was Feb. 22; Velma's was Oct. 12. If one of them had received a raise, they ordered omelettes with green peppers or green onions. Only once, when Velma won the lottery, did they order omelettes with cheese and bacon.

CHAPTER 7 GRAMMAR IQ QUIZ

Add commas where they are needed in the following sentences. Answers and explanations follow the quiz.

1. Janeece wanted to spend the summer abroad but she had to get at least a 3.5 grade point average for her parents to allow it.
2. Nick invited his brother his best friend and his girlfriend to the game.
3. My new apartment is located at 66 Baltic Street Brooklyn New York and will be available on November 1 2005.
4. Jeremy has long lean runner's legs.
5. I practiced a lot for the tournament but didn't make it past the second round.

Answers

1. Janeece wanted to spend the summer abroad, but she had to get at least a 3.5 grade point average for her parents to allow it. (separates two independent clauses separated by a conjunction)
2. Nick invited his brother, his best friend, and his girlfriend to the game. (separates items in a series)
3. My new apartment is located at 66 Baltic Street, Brooklyn, New York, and will be available on November 1, 2005. (separates items in an address and a date)
4. Jeremy has long, lean runner's legs. (separates two equally important adjectives)
5. I practiced a lot for the tournament, but didn't make it past the second round. (separates two contrasting ideas)

CHAPTER

7

MORE JOBS FOR COMMAS

Besides being road signs for sentences, commas also have many other jobs. This chapter explains other uses for commas and reviews what you learned about them in Chapter 6.

Grammar concepts to know:

- **items in a series**—a list of three or more similar words, phrases, or clauses
- **contrasting sentence elements**—two opposing ideas presented next to each other in a sentence

As you know, commas are used to separate sentence parts to make the meaning of the sentence clear. In this chapter, you'll learn how to use commas to separate independent clauses, items in a series, items in a date or address, adjectives, contrasting elements, and words that interrupt the flow of thought in a sentence. You'll also learn how to use commas in a friendly letter.

SEPARATING INDEPENDENT CLAUSES

You already know that an independent clause is a group of words that could stand alone as a complete sentence. A conjunction is a joining word. Here is a complete list of conjunctions that can be used to join two independent clauses:

and	*for*	*so*
but	*nor*	*yet*
or		

When two or more independent clauses are joined with a conjunction to make a compound sentence, a comma should follow the first clause. The commas and conjunctions are bolded in the following examples.

I knew I would win**, but** I didn't want to appear too eager.
Aisha studied Spanish in college**, so** she decided to spend a year in Spain after she graduated.
Eta wanted to order Italian food**, and** Jenna wanted Japanese.

If independent clauses are joined **without** a conjunction, they are separated by a semicolon instead of a comma.

I asked my boss if I could take my vacation in September**;** he said that he preferred I take it in October.
Josh is defending his thesis in the spring**;** I plan on going to see him do it.
Mihal is not sure what she wants to do after she graduates from college**;** she is thinking of becoming a marine biologist.

Practice

Use commas and semicolons to correctly punctuate the following sentences. Check your work with the answers at the end of the chapter. The changes are boldfaced for you.

1. Isaac started mowing the yard but his father finished it.
2. If you know of a good landscaper please give me the name of the company.
3. The furniture was covered with sheets yet it still became dusty and dirty.
4. Wayne likes Mike Oldfield he's an old New Age musician who's recorded a CD.

5. Edward knows what you want he just doesn't know where to find it.
6. Great things happen when we put our heads together.
7. The pilot was overcome with grief after the accident and he refused to fly again.
8. As you grow older your body absorbs fewer nutrients so many people take vitamin and mineral supplements.

SEPARATING ITEMS IN A SERIES

Separating a list of three or more similar words, phrases, or clauses makes the material easier for the reader to understand. Usually, the last item in a series is preceded by a conjunction. A comma is not required before the conjunction. However, some writers prefer to use one.

> Cory, Sue, John, and Craig went to the conference.
> The horse snorted, pawed the dirt, reared up, and ran off toward the hills.
> Sean taught me how to inventory the equipment, stock the shelves, and complete a quality-control check.

If each item in the series is separated by a conjunction, no commas are needed.

> Kara and Farrah and Andrea left their books behind.

SEPARATING ITEMS IN DATES AND ADDRESSES

When a year is specified in a date including the month and year, surround it with commas. If only the month or the season is listed, commas are not needed.

> Jody came to Fargo on June 1, 1997, right after she graduated from high school.
> Jody came to Fargo in June 1997 after graduating from high school.

When the name of a state is included to further identify a city, set it off with commas.

> Gail has lived in Peoria since last year.
> Gail has lived in Peoria, Illinois, since last year.

Practice

Add commas and endmarks where they are needed in the following sentences. Remember what you learned in the last chapter about commas. Check your work with the answers at the end of the chapter. The changes are boldfaced for you.

9. Sally bought a kitchen table Hal bought an iron a toaster a blender and gas grill

10. Seeing no answer to the problem Jeff quit for the day and went home

11. Bernice was born November 3 1928 and Eugene was born January 17 1929

12. The gentleman living at 547 35th Street St. Louis Missouri collects oak barrels pickling crocks and colored glass jars

13. After running into a police car with his truck Adam used his cellular phone to call the police his doctor his lawyer and his insurance agent

SEPARATING EQUALLY IMPORTANT ADJECTIVES

An **adjective** is a word that modifies, or describes, a noun or pronoun. Adjectives answer the questions *Which one? What kind?* and *How many?* The bolded words in the following sentences are adjectives.

> Kathy liked the **friendly, talkative, pleasant** boy sitting next to her at work. (The bolded words describe boy. They answer the question What kind?)

> The workmen repaired the floor with **that dark, aged oak** flooring. (The bolded words describe *flooring*. They answer the questions *Which one?* and *What kind?*)

> The reporter spoke with **several intense, talented high school** athletes. (The bolded words describe *athletes*. They answer the questions *How many?* and *What kind?)*

When adjectives are equally important in describing a word, they are separated by a comma. However, not all adjectives are equally important. Some adjectives must be right next to the word they modify, or they will not make sense. For instance, in the second example sentence above, the word *oak* must be placed next to the word *flooring*.

Pay close attention to the last example sentence above. The words *several, high,* and *school* are all adjectives modifying *athletes,* but they are not separated by commas. These adjectives need to stay where they are in the sentence for the words to make sense, and they should not be separated by a comma from the word they modify. Only adjectives of equal importance are set off by a comma.

How can you tell if adjectives should be separated with a comma? Apply one or both of these tests:

1. Change the order of the adjectives. If the sentence reads just as clearly, separate the adjectives with a comma. If the sentence becomes unclear or sounds awkward, do not use a comma. The first example sentence on the previous page makes sense even if the position of the adjectives is changed.

   In the last example sentence, the sentence would make no sense if the adjectives came in this order: *intense, several, high, talented, school. Intense* and *talented* are the only adjectives in the sentence that can be reversed; therefore, they are the only adjectives separated by a comma.

   Alex liked the **pleasant, friendly, talkative** boy sitting next to him at work.
   The carpenter repaired the floor with that **aged, dark** oak flooring.
   The reporter spoke with several **talented, intense** high school athletes.

2. A second, equally effective test is to place the word *and* between the adjectives. If the sentence still reads well, use commas between the adjectives. If the sentence sounds unclear or awkward, do not use commas. Again, this works with the first two example sentences, but in the last sentence, an *and* makes sense only between *intense* and *talented.*

   Alex liked the **friendly and talkative and pleasant** boy sitting next to him at work.
   The carpenter repaired the floor with that **dark and aged** oak flooring.
   The reporter spoke with several **intense and talented** high school athletes.

Practice

Try these two tests with the following sentences. Where do the commas belong?

14. Marshall cut his short wavy light blond hair.
15. In my wallet are five crisp new twenty dollar bills.

SEPARATING SENTENCE ELEMENTS

- Use commas to separate contrasting elements in a sentence. The following examples illustrate contrasting elements in a sentence. The comma tells the reader that what follows is an opposite idea. It makes the idea easier for the reader to grasp. The contrasting ideas are bolded.

  I interviewed well, **but did poorly on the written test.**
  This company needs problem solvers, **not complainers**, to tackle our challenges.
  The liquid poured slowly at first, **quickly toward the end.**
  The tour group expected to meet the actors, **not a press agent.**

- Use commas to separate words or phrases that interrupt the flow of thought in a sentence. In the following examples, words and phrases that interrupt the flow of thought have been bolded.

  The task, **it seemed to us**, was overwhelming.
  The dog remembered, **however**, the harsh words and cruel actions of his owner.
  Morning, **we discovered**, was the best time to water the lawn.

- Whenever the name of the person being addressed is included in a sentence, it should be set off by commas. Jessi is the person being addressed in each of the following examples. Notice how commas are used to set off her name, depending on where it is placed in the sentence.

  Jessi, Pat needs you to sign for a package in the office before you leave.
  Pat needs you to sign for a package in the office, **Jessi**, before you leave.
  Pat needs you to sign for a package in the office before you leave, **Jessi.**

- Mild exclamations included in a sentence are also set off with commas. The exclamations have been bolded for you in each of the following examples.

  Gosh, I never expected you'd make such a fuss.
  No, we won't be needing you any longer.
  Heck, we could have done that hours ago.

USING COMMAS IN A FRIENDLY LETTER

- Use a comma after the greeting of a friendly letter.

Dear Aunt Hilda,
Dear Juanita,
Dear Val,

- Use a comma after the closing of a friendly letter.

Sincerely yours,
Yours truly,

Practice

Using what you have learned so far about commas and semicolons, correct these sentences. Check your work with the corrected versions of the sentences at the end of the chapter.

16. Exhausted from sitting rather than from physical exertion Ling sank into the soft green easy chair.
17. The Founders Day sale runs December 26 2005 through January 8 2006.
18. Suddenly the rope tore and the tire swing plummeted to the ground.
19. We're sorry Tom that you were inconvenienced and we'd like to make it up to you.
20. The new address if I'm remembering correctly is 1140 Westown Cole Illinois.
21. When I travel I pack my toothbrush a hairbrush a shoe brush and a clothes brush.
22. Yes the sales department met their monthly goal over $200,000 in receipts they're celebrating right now!

Answers

1. Isaac started mowing the yard, but his father finished it.
2. If you know of a good landscaper, please give me the name of the company.
3. The furniture was covered with sheets, yet it still became dusty and dirty.
4. Wayne likes Mike Oldfield; he's an old New Age musician who's recorded a CD.
5. Edward knows what you want; he just doesn't know where to find it.

6. No change.

7. The pilot was overcome with grief after the accident, and he refused to fly again.

8. As you grow older, your body absorbs fewer nutrients, so many people take vitamin and mineral supplements.

9. Sally bought a kitchen table, Hal bought an iron, a toaster, a blender, and gas grill.

10. Seeing no answer to the problem, Jeff quit for the day and went home.

11. Bernice was born November 3, 1928, and Eugene was born January 17, 1929.

12. The gentleman living at 547 35th Street, St. Louis, Missouri, collects oak barrels, pickling crocks, and colored glass jars.

13. After running into a police car with his truck, Adam used his cellular phone to call the police, his doctor, his lawyer, and his insurance agent.

14. Marshall cut his short, wavy light blond hair.

15. In my wallet are five crisp, new twenty dollar bills.

16. Exhausted from sitting, rather than the phsyical exertion, Ling sank into th soft, gren easy chair.

17. The Founders Day sale runs December 26, 2005, through January 8, 2006.

18. Suddenly, the rope tore, and the tire swing plummeted to the ground.

19. We're sorry, Tom, that you were inconvenienced, and we'd like to make it up to you.

20. The new address, if I'm remembering correctly, is 1140 Westown, Cole, Illinois.

21. When I travel, I pack my toothbrush, a hairbrush, a shoe brush, and a clothes brush.

22. Yes, the sales department met their monthly goal, over $200,000 in receipts; they're celebrating right now!

CHAPTER 8 GRAMMAR IQ QUIZ

Add commas, semicolons, and colons wherever they are needed in the following sentences. Answers and explanations follow the quiz.

1. Your budget is gone you need to stop spending money.
2. The results of the tests were inconclusive therefore the group decided to gather more information.
3. The charter trip includes stops in Denver Colorado Salt Lake City Utah Reno Nevada and Portland Oregon.
4. These items are essential for fishing a tackle box a life jacket and a good fishing pole.
5. At 12 23 P.M. the book *Standing on the Edge A Closer Look at Mountain Climbing* goes on sale.

Answers

1. Your budget is gone; you need to stop spending money. (Semicolon separates two independent clauses joined without a conjunction.)
2. The results of the tests were inconclusive; therefore, the group decided to gather more information. (Semicolon precedes a conjunctive adverb; a comma follows it.)
3. The charter trip includes stops in Denver, Colorado; Salt Lake City, Utah; Reno, Nevada; and Portland, Oregon.
4. These items are essential for fishing: a tackle box, a life jacket, and a good fishing pole.
5. At 12:23 P.M., the book *Standing on the Edge: A Closer Look at Mountain Climbing* goes on sale.

CHAPTER

GETTING FANCY WITH SEMICOLONS AND COLONS

Semicolons (;) and colons (:) confuse many writers. This chapter sorts it all out for you. By the time you finish, you'll know exactly how to use both.

Grammar concepts to know:

- **subordinating conjunction**—a word such as *because*, *although*, *if*, *when*, etc., that introduces a dependent clause
- **conjunctive adverb**—a word such as *consequently*, *however*, *therefore*, etc., that separates two related independent clauses

In this chapter, you will review what you have learned about punctuation so far, especially the use of semicolons to separate independent clauses. You will also learn how to use semicolons with certain joining words, and when to separate items in a series with semicolons. Finally, you will learn some of the uses of colons.

SEMICOLONS

Separating Independent Clauses

- Use a semicolon to separate independent clauses joined without a conjunction. This rule may seem familiar because it was also included in Chapters 4 and 7. Refresh your memory with these example sentences.

  I chose Ben as my partner; we are an undefeatable team.
  Kara cooked dinner; I bought the groceries.
  You worked hard for this; your reward is well deserved.

- Use a semicolon to separate independent clauses that contain commas, even if the clauses are joined by a conjunction.

  Danny likes doing bench presses, arm curls, leg extensions, and other weight-training exercises; but Jen prefers cardiovascular training.

  In this sentence, the semicolon helps the reader see where the break in thought occurs. The semicolon makes the sentence easier to understand.

- Use a semicolon to separate independent clauses connected with a conjunctive adverb that expresses a relationship between clauses (see Chapter 4). When these words (such as *however, therefore, then,* and *thus*) connect two independent clauses, the first independent clause is followed by a semicolon, and the conjunctive adverb is followed by a comma. Look at the following examples to see how this is done.

  I lost my job; **therefore,** I had to cancel my trip to Europe.
  Noah wanted to spend four months living abroad; **however,** he couldn't get a visa that let him stay more than three months.
  I decided against going to Greece; **instead,** I chose to visit Costa Rica.
  Carla began studying Japanese to prepare for her trip; **furthermore,** she signed up for an Asian history course.

Here is a list of these conjuctive adverbs:

accordingly	*however*	*then*
besides	*instead*	*therefore*
consequently	*moreover*	*thus*
furthermore	*nevertheless*	
hence	*otherwise*	

It's easy to confuse these conjunctive adverbs with subordinating conjunctions such as *because, although, since, until,* and *while.* Subordinating conjunctions introduce dependent clauses that cannot stand alone as a sentence. The conjunctive adverbs, however, introduce independent clauses that can stand alone, with or without the adverb.

Here's an easy test to see if the word beginning a clause is a subordinating conjunction, for which you need only a comma, or a conjunctive adverb that needs a semicolon: If you can move the word around in the clause, it's a conjunctive adverb, the joining word that takes a semicolon. If not, it's probably a subordinating conjunction. Let's try the test with these two independent clauses:

> My paycheck was late. I couldn't pay my rent on time.

Here are two different ways of combining these two independent clauses.

> My paycheck was late; therefore, I couldn't pay my rent on time.
> I couldn't pay my rent on time because my paycheck was late.

In the first sentence, you could move *therefore* to a different place in the clause if you wanted to. You could say, "I couldn't, therefore, pay my rent on time." So, *therefore* is a conjunctive adverb.

In the second sentence, the word *because* makes no sense anywhere else in the clause. You wouldn't say, "My paycheck because was late." Therefore, *because* is a subordinate conjunction.

Separating Items in a Series

Use a semicolon to separate items in a series that contain commas. This helps the reader see which sets of items go together. Unlike items in a series separated by commas, a semicolon is used even when there *is* a conjunction.

> The possible dates for the potluck are Thursday, June 5; Saturday, June 7; Sunday, June 8; or Monday, June 9.
> On our team you'll find the hustlers, Jake and Marilynn; the slackers, Henrietta, Chuck, and Kerald; and the easy-going people, Judy, Rob, and Kirsten.
> The packing plant will relocate to either Fort Madison, Iowa; Omaha, Nebraska; or Sioux Falls, South Dakota.

Practice

Use what you have learned to add commas and semicolons to the following sentences. Check your work with the answers at the end of the chapter. The changes are boldfaced for you.

1. Helen left her desk unlocked at work consequently she worried about it all night.
2. The menu included broiled salmon steamed broccoli grilled potatoes spinach and bread but for some reason they served no dessert.
3. Tim hurried through his work however he still wasn't finished by 8:30.
4. The bus traveled through Chicago Illinois Dayton Ohio and Pittsburgh Pennsylvania.
5. I've been at this for two days I need to get away for a while.

COLONS

Colons That Introduce

- Use a colon to introduce a list of items.

  These people were transferred: Audrey, Brett, Bradley, and Lindsay.
  We ordered the following supplies: paper, staplers, scissors, markers, and tape.

  Do not use a colon if the list of items completes the meaning begun by the verb, in other words, if it fits right into the flow of the sentence. Here are the previous example sentences, rewritten in such a way that a colon is not necessary.

  The people transferred were Audrey, Brett, Bradley, and Lindsay.
  We ordered paper, staplers, scissors, markers, and tape.

- Use a colon to introduce a formal quotation.

  Nietzsche offered this sound advice: "Smash not the happy delusions of men."

- Use a colon to introduce a word, phrase, or clause that adds particular emphasis to the main body of a sentence.

  Your busy work schedule is the result of one thing: poor planning.
  Jerry needed one peice of essential information: the price.

Colons That Show Relationship

Use a colon to show a relationship in the following cases:

- Between two independent clauses when the second explains the first.

  Judy shouted and turned cartwheels: She had just finished the last page of the report.
  Brian framed the paycheck: It was the first check he had ever earned.
  Sylvia ignored the doorbell: She knew it was a salesman she had no time for.

- Between the title and the subtitle of a book.

  Measurement: Translating into Metric
  Next Step: A Futuristic View of Technology
  Fear: Tales from the Dark Side

- Between volumes and page numbers.

  Contemporary Authors V:128
  Education Digest 10:23
  Marvel Comics 21:24

- Between chapters and verses.

  James 3:10
  Exodus 1:1
  Proverbs 2:2

- Between hours and minutes.

  12:53 A.M.
  2:10 P.M.

USING COLONS IN BUSINESS LETTERS

You learned in Chapter 7 that a comma follows the greeting (or salutation) in a personal, or friendly, letter. In business communications, a colon signals the reader that what follows is a business matter, something to be taken seriously. This is particularly true if you include the position, but not the name of the person to whom the letter is addressed. However, even in a business letter, the closing is followed by a comma.

Dear Ms. Essian:
Sincerely yours,

Dear Editor:
Cordially yours,

Practice

Practice what you have learned about commas, semicolons, and colons by adding them to the following sentences. Check your work with the answers. The changes that follow are boldfacd for you.

6. Hammond located the procedure in the policy manual Volume 6 89.

7. The hail destroyed all of the wheat however the corn was untouched by the violent storm.

8. Before I bought a new car I did some research in the library checked out the local car dealerships asked a few friends for advice and consulted my mechanic.

9. Dear Customer

Your order should arrive on or before January 5 2006.

Sincerely yours

10. Each day a new shift begins at 8 30 A.M. 4 30 P.M. and 12 30 A.M.

11. Megan likes to play soccer a physically challenging sport bridge a game of logic and strategy Street Fighter a mindless PS2 game and the harmonica an invigorating instrument.

12. The police learned the following information from the interrogation the suspect's name his home address his phone number and his current employer.

Answers

1. Helen left her desk unlocked at work; consequently, she worried about it all night.

2. The menu included broiled salmon, steamed broccoli, grilled potatoes, spinach, and bread; but for some reason, they served no dessert.

3. Tim hurried through his work; however, he still wasn't finished by 8:00.

4. The bus traveled through Chicago, Illinois; Dayton, Ohio; and Pittsburgh, Pennsylvania.

5. I've been at this for two days; I need to get away for a while.

6. Hammond located the procedure in the policy manual Volume 6:89.

7. The hail destroyed all of the wheat; however, the corn was untouched by the violent storm.

8. Before I bought a new car, I did some research in the library, checked out the local car dealerships, asked a few friends for advice, and consulted my mechanic.

9. Dear Customer:

Your order should arrive on or before January 5, 2006.

Sincerely yours,

10. Each day, a new shift begins at 8:30 A.M., 4:30 P.M., and 12:30 A.M.

11. Megan likes to play soccer, a physically challenging sport; bridge, a game of logic and strategy; Street Fighter, a mindless PS2 game; and the harmonica, an invigorating instrument.

12. The police learned the following information from the interrogation: the suspect's name, his home address, his phone number, and his current employer.

CHAPTER 9 GRAMMAR IQ QUIZ

Add quotation marks wherever they are needed in the following sentences. Answers and explanations follow the quiz.

1. The teacher called him a poor excuse for a student.
2. If you shovel the drive, Mom said, I'll make hot chocolate.
3. The short story was entitled The Tell-Tale Heart.
4. The hinges are defective, said Josh. Let's remove them.
5. We saw Fear Factor last night.

Answers

1. The teacher called him a "poor excuse for a student." (surrounds directly quoted words)
2. "If you shovel the drive," Mom said, "I'll make hot chocolate." (encloses exact words in a conversation)
3. The short story was entitled "The Tell-Tale Heart." (surrounds the title of a short story)
4. "The hinges are defective," said Josh. "Let's remove them." (encloses exact words in a conversation)
5. We saw "Fear Factor" last night. (surrounds the title of a TV show)

CHAPTER

CONTROLLING QUOTATION MARKS

This chapter explains the knotty problems of quotation marks, both double and single. By the time you finish, you'll be in control of quotation marks in your writing.

Grammar concepts to know:

- **direct quotation**—someone's exact written, spoken, or inscribed words
- **paraphrase**—a restatement of a direct quotation
- **slang**—highly informal language used only in informal conversation

Quotation marks pose a problem for many writers, but a few simple rules can make them easy to use. Although these marks are most often found in dialogue, other writing situations require them as well.

USING QUOTATION MARKS IN DIRECT QUOTATIONS

- Use double quotation marks to set off a direct quotation or thought within a sentence or paragraph. This includes quotations that are signed, etched, inscribed, carved, and so on.

  The managers called our new pricing policy "the innovation of the decade."

We thought he said, "Turn right at the corner."
The sign read, "No Smoking."
"Eccentric and Erratic," the headstone read.

- Do not use quotation marks for a paraphrase, or the restatement of a direct quotation or thought in other words. The following examples illustrate the difference.

The teacher said, "Turn your papers in at the end of class." (direct quotation)
The teacher said to turn our papers in at the end of class. (paraphrase)

"Why can't I shake this flu?" I wondered. (direct thought)
I wondered why I couldn't shake this flu. (paraphrase of a thought)

The sign clearly read, "No parking." (signed words)
The sign said not to park. (paraphrase)

- Use single quotation marks to set off a quotation within a quotation.

"Beth couldn't make it, so she told me, 'I'll catch up with you later,'" said Grace.
The sales manager said, "The attitude of my most successful salesman is: 'No job is too big or small.'"
My doctor always says, "Take my wife's advice: 'If it tastes good, it has to be fattening!'"

USING QUOTATION MARKS IN DIALOGUE

Correctly punctuating dialogue means understanding how to use quotation marks, commas, and endmarks. Take a close look at the sentences in the following dialogue sample: They include the basic dialogue structures. The words quoted are called **quotations**, and the words explaining who said the quotations are called **tags**. In these examples, the tags are in bold.

"I'm really hungry. I want something to eat," **said Harry.**
Nina answered, "I'm hungry, but I don't have any cash. Do you have some?"

"What is this?" **Harry asked.** "You're the one with the manager's job."
"Yes," **Nina said,** "but credit cards are all I ever carry."

Quoted words are always surrounded by quotation marks. Place quotation marks before a group of quoted words and again at the end. Tags are punctuated differently depending on where they are in the sentence.

- If the tag follows a quotation, and the quotation is a sentence normally ending with a period, use a comma instead. The period comes at the end of the tag. (See the first example sentence, on the previous page.)

  However, if the quotation is a sentence normally ending with a question mark or an exclamation point, insert the question mark or exclamation point. Place a period after the tag, but do not use a comma. The examples that follow illustrate these rules.

  "I'm really tired of driving. Let's find a hotel," said Aaron.
  "I'm really tired of driving. Do you want to find a hotel?" asked Aaron.
  "I'm really tired of driving. Wait—there's a Holiday Inn!" exclaimed Aaron.

- When the tag comes before the quotation, place a comma after the tag. Put quotation marks around the quoted words, capitalize the first word of the quotation, and punctuate the sentence as you would normally. See how this is shown in these sentences.

  Aaron said, "I'm really tired of driving. Let's find a hotel."
  Aaron said, "I'm really tired of driving. Do you want to find a hotel?"
  Aaron said, "I'm really tired of driving. Wait—there's a Holiday Inn!"

- Sometimes, the tag interrupts the quotation. If both the first and second parts of the quotation are complete sentences, the first part of the quotation is punctuated in the same way as a quotation with the tag at the end. In other words, the period follows the tag. The rest of the quotation is punctuated in the same way as a quotation preceded by a tag. See the following example sentences.

  "I'm really tired of driving," said Aaron. "Let's find a hotel."
  "I'm really tired of driving," said Aaron. "Do you want to find a hotel?"
  "I'm really tired of driving, said Aaron. "Wait—a Holiday Inn!"

- When the tag interrupts a sentence, the words preceding the tag begin the thought, and the words following the tag complete the thought. Place quotation marks around the quoted words and follow the first part of the quotation with a comma. Place a comma after the tag—not a period since the sentence is not completed. Place quotation marks around the last part of the quotation, but *do not* capitalize the first letter of the quotation as it is not the beginning of a new sentence. Punctuate the rest of the sentence as you would normally. See the example sentences below.

> "The Carters just don't understand," observed Solomon, "why they upset you so."
>
> "This lawn care service," explained Alvin, "provides fertilizer, seed, and weed control."
>
> "What I can't see," mused Mel, "is what you see in him."

Note: All of the punctuation is *inside* the quotation marks except for the punctuation marks following the tags.

Dialogue at a Glance

- Tags following a quotation:
  "__________________," said Rose.
  "__________________?" asked Rose.
  "__________________!" exclaimed Rose.

- Tags preceding a quotation:
  Iris said, "__________________."
  Iris asked, "__________________?"
  Iris exclaimed, "__________________!"

- Tags between two sentences of a quotation:
  "____________," said Lily. "____________."
  "____________?" asked Lily. "____________?"
  "____________!" exclaimed Lily. "____________!"

- Tags interrupting a one-sentence quotation:
  "____________," said Daisy, "____________."
  "____________," asked Daisy, "____________?"
  "____________," exclaimed Daisy, "____________!"

OTHER USES FOR QUOTATION MARKS

- Use quotation marks to set off nicknames and words used as slang.

  Kristy was dubbed "speed demon" by her teammates.
  All the kids said the new CD was really "bad."

- Use quotation marks to indicate irony or raised eyebrows. Avoid overusing quotation marks in this way. It doesn't work if you do it all the time.

  My yearly "evaluation" involved a three-minute conversation with the boss.
  That "consultant" offered no advice or counsel.
  Their idea of a "good time" is doing laundry.

- Use quotation marks to set off titles of certain items. Other titles should be italicized. The following table shows these differences.

Enclose in Quotation Marks	**Italicize**
name of a short story or chapter of a book	title of a novel
name of a TV program title of a poem	name of a movie title of a collection of poetry or an epic poem
headline of an article or title of a report title of a song	name of a magazine or newspaper title of a musical or long musical composition
	name of a ship, plane, train, etc.

Italics instead of Quotation Marks

Italics are used instead of quotation marks for titles of the items in the second column of the table above. They are also used when referring to words as words, and for emphasis:

Words as words:

The word *food* always brought a smile to his face.

Emphasis:

I have *never* seen anyone so fond of music.

Quotation Marks with Other Punctuation Marks

Here are the rules for combining quotation marks with other punctuation marks:

- Question marks, exclamation points, and dashes go *inside* quotation marks if they are part of a quotation. If they are not, place them *outside* the quotation marks.

 The dentist asked, "Can you feel sensitivity in this area?" (part of the quotation)
 Did you watch last week's "Lost"? (not part of the quotation)
 "I wish I'd never heard of—" Calvin stopped suddenly as Kelly entered the room. (part of the quotation)
 My favorite song will always be "The Rose"! (not part of the quotation)

- Periods and commas go *inside* closing quotation marks.

 "Wait for half an hour," suggested Dalia, "before you go swimming."

- Colons and semicolons go *outside* closing quotation marks.

 Here's how I felt about last week's "Friends": I loved it.
 The interviewer dismissed the remark as a "slip of the tongue"; the guest was insulted.

Practice

Use what you have learned about quotation marks to correct the following sentences. Check your work with the answers that follow.

1. Do you ever watch CSI on CBS? asked Steven.
2. Which one of you called me a cowardly excuse for a soldier? barked the sergeant.
3. After reading To Kill a Mockingbird, I rented the movie.
4. An extra five minutes at lunch was our prize.
5. All the teenagers at the party were duded out.
6. If you want to know why I'm so bitter, read my article Rosy Glasses in the latest copy of our newsletter, The Tower.
7. I wish that old fussbudget—Melanie stopped abruptly as Mr. Harris walked into the room.

8. Do you call everyone by the name Bubba asked Katie.
9. The investigator asked us where we had spent the evening.
10. Don't make outrageous excuses my attorney advised that will only make matters worse.
11. Ebenezer said I told you the representative said No way before I ever had a chance to explain.
12. Why are you still here my supervisor asked everyone else went home an hour ago.
13. We were shocked by our Christmas bonus a bag with a cookie and an orange.
14. Looking at her tardy record, I see why you've named her Punctual Paula.
15. Get out of the way yelled the captain.

Answers

1. "Do you ever watch 'CSI' on CBS?" asked Steven.
2. "Which one of you called me a 'cowardly excuse for a soldier'?" barked the sergeant.
3. After reading *To Kill a Mockingbird,* I rented the movie.
4. An extra five minutes at lunch was our "prize."
5. All the teenagers at the party were "duded out."
6. If you want to know why I'm so bitter, read my article "Rosy Glasses" in the latest copy of our newsletter, *The Tower.*
7. "I wish that old fussbudget—" Melanie stopped abruptly as Mr. Harris walked into the room.
8. "Do you call everyone by the name 'Bubba'?" asked Katie.
9. No change.
10. "Don't make outrageous excuses," my attorney advised. "That will only make matters worse."
11. Ebenezer said, "I told you the representative said, 'No way!' before I ever had a chance to explain."
12. "Why are you still here?" my supervisor asked. "Everyone else went home an hour ago."
13. We were shocked by our Christmas "bonus": a bag with a cookie and an orange.
14. Looking at her tardy record, I see why you've named her "Punctual Paula."
15. "Get out of the way!" yelled the captain.

CHAPTER 10 GRAMMAR IQ QUIZ

Add apostrophes and dashes wherever they are needed in the following sentences. Answers and explanations follow the quiz.

1. The manager evaluated the sales associates performance.
2. The fine equaled two weeks pay.
3. Owen isnt scheduled to work today.
4. Marianna is disappointed we are too that the performance was canceled.
5. Preparation and hard work these are the keys to successfully implementing a plan.

Answers

1. The manager evaluated the sales associate's performance. (apostrophe shows possession)
2. The fine equaled two weeks' pay. (shows possession)
3. Owen isn't scheduled to work today. (apostrophe denotes a contraction)
4. Marianna is disappointed—we are too—that the performance was canceled. (marks a sudden break in thought)
5. Preparation and hard work—these are the keys to successfully implementing a plan. (connects a beginning phrase to the rest of the sentence)

CHAPTER 10 THE MYSTERIES OF APOSTROPHES AND DASHES

This chapter puts you in command of apostrophes and dashes, the most commonly misused punctuation marks.

Grammar concept to know:

- **contraction**—two words condensed into one word with an apostrophe *(will not = won't; did not = didn't)*

Apostrophes communicate important information in written language. Dashes, when used sparingly, add emphasis. The first part of this chapter covers the rules regarding apostrophes. The last part covers dashes.

APOSTROPHES

Using Apostrophes to Show Possession

Apostrophes are used to show that one or more things belong to one or more people or things. Apostrophes are often used because they shorten sentences, meaning fewer words for the reader. The following sets of examples illustrate this.

> These books belong to the girl.
> These are the **girl's** books.

We must update the computer system of the hospital.
We must update the **hospital's** computer system.

I need to switch the veterinarian of my dog.
I need to switch my **dog's** veterinarian.

Changing the location of an apostrophe can change the meaning of a sentence. Look at each of the following sentences. The words in parentheses explain what the apostrophe means.

These are the **girl's** books. (The books belong to one girl.)
These are the **girls'** books. (The books belong to more than one girl.)

We must update the **hospital's** computer system. (This is referring to the computer system of one hospital.)
We must update the **hospitals'** computer system. (This is referring to the computer system of more than one hospital.)

I need to switch my **dog's** veterinarian. (This is referring to the veterinarian of one dog.)
I need to switch my **dogs'** veterinarian. (This is referring to the veterinarian of more than one dog.)

The position of the apostrophe tells the reader whether one person or thing possesses something, or if it's more than one person or thing doing the possessing. That is, it tells whether the word that possesses is singular (referring to one) or plural (referring to more than one).

- Add **'s** to singular words not ending in *s*.

cat's toy
queen's throne
physician's assistant
book's cover

- Add **'s** to singular words ending in *s*.

Garth **Brooks's** latest recording
American **Express's** advertising campaign
Lois's birth certificate

- Add **s'** to plural words ending in *s*.

 girls' bicycles
 kids' books
 ladies' garments
 employees' agreement

- Add **'s** to plural words not ending in *s*.

 women's plans
 children's bedrooms
 men's shoes
 people's election

When a common or proper noun is more than one word, special rules apply. Usually, you add the *'s* to the last word in the noun

- Add **'s** to the last word of a compound noun.

 mother-in-law's visit
 president-elect's decision
 manager-in-training's duties

- Add **'s** to the last word of the name of a business or institution.

 Proctor and **Gamble's** products
 First State **Bank's** new hours
 Banton and Barton **Co.'s** president

- Add **'s** to the last name mentioned if a single item belongs to more than one person.

 Wayne and **Judy's** log home
 the receptionist and **secretary's** printer
 Mr. and Mrs. **Mitchell's** car

- Add an apostrophe to words showing periods of time if they show possession.

  one **day's** schedule
  one **year's** salary
  three **days'** wait

- Add an apostrophe to words showing amounts of money if they show possession.

  two **cents'** worth
  a **dollar's** serial number
  a **penny's** value

Using Apostrophes to Show Omission

Use an apostrophe to show that letters or numbers have been omitted.

Becky **doesn't** (does not) work today.
The doctor **couldn't** (could not) give me a prescription.
Who's (who is) on first?
I **can't** (cannot) get together tomorrow afternoon.
My first car was a **'67** (1967) Chevy.
Uncle Louis tells lies about life in the **'50s** (1950s).

When Not to Use Apostrophes

- Do not use an apostrophe to form a plural, but only to show possession for either singular or plural words.

  Wrong: Get the tomatoe's from the garden.
  Correct: Trim the **tomatoes'** lower limbs.

  Wrong: Read the nutrition label on this bag of chip's.
  Correct: Read the bag of **chips'** nutrition label.

- Do not use an apostrophe with words that already show possession (*my, mine, our, ours, your, yours, his, her, hers, their, theirs*). Note that these words do not have apostrophes in the following examples.

  This is their boat. The boat is **theirs**. (no apostrophe)
  We brought our grill. The grill is **ours**. (no apostrophe)
  This experiment must be **yours**. (no apostrophe)

Practice

Practice what you have learned about apostrophes and other punctuation marks to correct the following sentences. Check your work with the answers at the end of the chapter.

1. Mr. Jones grocery store has better produce than Mrs. Smiths.
2. Comp USAs top-selling product is Microns latest MMX computer.
3. Janices and Jays horse was named the Grand Champion Stud.
4. After six weeks steady work we earn a permanent position and a days paid vacation.
5. The picnic basket is their's.
6. Our firms territory has doubled in the last six months and the new responsibility is your's.
7. Every Saturday afternoon the Womens Issues Group meets for lunch.
8. Bonnie works as a dentists assistant.
9. Employees motivations differ from an owners.
10. A managers reward is different from an employees.

DASHES

A dash is a specialized punctuation mark reserved for only a few types of situations. However, many writers use it incorrectly. Dashes call attention to themselves. Because of this, a careful writer uses them sparingly. They are very effective if used correctly, but they lose their impact if they are overused.

- Use a dash to mark a sudden break in thought or to insert a comment.

    Take these files and this—Look out for that truck!
    I remember the day—what teenager doesn't—that the space shuttle exploded.
    Abby is delighted—as we are—about your new job.

- Use a dash to emphasize explanatory material. You don't have to use a dash, but you may.

    Realizing your limitations—time, money, and energy—makes planning more realistic.
    He lit a cigarette inside the building—an unconscious habit.

- Use a dash to indicate omitted letters.

  "Oh, d—, I lost the code for the copier!"
  He had received a letter from Mrs. N—.

- Use a dash to connect a beginning phrase to the rest of the sentence.

  Diversity and challenge—these are the advantages of our new programming.
  Albany, New York, and Trenton, New Jersey—that's where our current staff will be relocating.

Practice

Use what you know about dashes to correctly punctuate the following sentences. Check your work with the answers at the end of the chapter.

11. To run or to hide those were her only choices.
12. Our idea just in case you're interested is to remove the plastic coating.
13. Mr. O'Dea is the most unreasonable I should keep my opinions to myself.
14. I can never find his d pocket organizer when he Oh, now I've got it.
15. Intelligence, perseverance, and luck that's what you'll need for this job.

REVIEW

Practice what you have learned about punctuation so far by adding capitalization, endmarks, commas, semicolons, colons, apostrophes, and dashes to the following sentences. Check your work on these complicated sentences with the corrected versions on the next page.

16. though it is hard to understand my partners purpose in interviewing dr e s sanders jr was to eliminate him as a suspect in the crime
17. before the ambulance reached the corner of woodland and vine ms anderson saw a dark hooded figure crawl through the window reach back grab a small parcel and run north on vine
18. as the detective interrogated each of the boys and their fathers they determined that the mens stories did not match up with the boys versions
19. please bring these items when you drive up here tomorrow barbaras sleeping bag another can of avon insect repellent the girls queen-sized air mattress they want to use it to sunbathe on the water and my swimming trunks
20. karl malone and john stockton these two made an exciting combination a mixture of malones aggressiveness and stocktons finesse

Answers

1. Mr. Jones's grocery store has better produce than Mrs. Smith's.
2. Comp USA's top-selling product is Micron's latest MMX computer.
3. Janice and Jay's horse was named the Grand Champion Stud.
4. After six weeks' steady work, we earn a permanent position and a day's paid vacation.
5. The picnic basket is theirs.
6. Our firm's territory has doubled in the last six months, and the new responsibility is yours.
7. Every Saturday afternoon, the Women's Issues Group meets for lunch.
8. Bonnie works as a dentist's assistant.
9. Employees' motivations differ from an owner's.
10. A manager's reward is different from an employee's.
11. To run or to hide—those were her only choices.
12. Our idea—just in case you're interested—is to remove the plastic coating.
13. Mr. O'Dea is the most unreasonable—I should keep my opinions to myself.
14. I can never find his d— pocket organizer when he—Oh, now I've got it.
15. Intelligence, perseverance, and luck—that's what you'll need for this job.
16. Though it is hard to understand, my partner's purpose in interviewing Dr. E.S. Sanders, Jr., was to eliminate him as a suspect in the crime.
17. Before the ambulance reached the corner of Woodland and Vine, Ms. Anderson saw a dark, hooded figure crawl through the window, reach back, grab a small parcel, and run north on Vine.
18. As the detectives interrogated each of the boys and their fathers, they determined that the men's stories did not match up with the boys' versions.
19. Please bring these items when you drive up here tomorrow: Barbara's sleeping bag, another can of Avon insect repellent, the girls' queen-sized air mattress—they want to use it to sunbathe on the water—and my swimming trunks.
20. Karl Malone and John Stockton—these two made an exciting combination, a mixture of Malone's aggressiveness and Stockton's finesse.

CHAPTER 11 GRAMMAR IQ QUIZ

Use parentheses, hyphens, slashes, and numbers correctly in the following sentences. Answers and explanations follow the quiz.

1. The secretary treasurer read the minutes from last month's meeting.
2. Madison Avenue the street one block east of our house is being resurfaced.
3. The parents of the sick child Otto and Rachel requested a second opinion.
4. Vegetables and or fruits are essential to healthy eating.
5. We ordered (12, twelve) jelly doughnuts.

Answers

1. The secretary-treasurer read the minutes from last month's meeting. (joins two words working as one)
2. Madison Avenue (the street one block east of our house) is being resurfaced. (encloses an explanation that interrupts the flow of a sentence)
3. The parents of the sick child (Otto and Rachel) requested a second opinion. (encloses information when accuracy is important)
4. Vegetables and/or fruits are essential to healthy eating. (shows that the sentence refers to one or both words)
5. We ordered twelve jelly doughnuts. (Write out a number that can be written as one or two words.)

THE FINER POINTS OF PUNCTUATION

Most people misuse hyphens once in a while. Parentheses and diagonal slashes also cause problems, littering your written work like blemishes on an otherwise smooth surface. This chapter explains when to use the less-often-used (and more often misused) punctuation marks and explains how to write numbers.

Grammar concepts to know:

- **hyphenated word**—two or more words joined by a hyphen to create a single word (*well-known*)
- **compound word**—two words joined together to form one (*cowboy, storeroom*)

The punctuation marks covered in this lesson—hyphens, parentheses, and diagonal marks—serve very specific purposes. Knowing and understanding their functions gives a writer an advantage in communicating ideas. This chapter explains how to use these marks. The last part of the chapter discusses using numbers in writing.

HYPHENS

The main purpose of a hyphen is to join words to create a compound word, which is a combination of words used as one word. Compound words may be written in three ways: as a single word, as two words, or as a hyphenated word. Whenever you are in doubt, consult a recent dictionary.

Since language changes constantly, a word written as two words often evolves into a hyphenated word, then eventually becomes a single word. For example, the word *semicolon* began as two separate words (*semi colon*). In the late fifties, dictionaries began listing it as a hyphenated word (*semi-colon*). A recent dictionary will list it as a single word (*semicolon*).

Two-Word Compound Nouns

couch potato
hat rack
window box
guitar pick

Hyphenated Compound Nouns

father-in-law
mayor-elect
cook-off
co-payment
light-year
ball-and-socket joint

Single-Word Compound Nouns

driveway
raindrop
candlelight
speedboat
sunscreen
watermelon

- Use a hyphen to join two words working together as one.

Mark is a **singer-dancer.**
Pete Rose was a **player-coach** for the Cincinnati Reds.
George Clooney has joined the ranks of well-known **actor-directors.**

- Use a hyphen to join more than two words into a single word.

  know-it-all
  good-for-nothing
  five-year-old

- Use a hyphen to join two or more words that function as a single modifying word. If the modifying words follow the word they modify, the modifying words are not hyphenated. Pay special attention to how these hyphenated adjectives are used when they follow the nouns they modify.

  An **ill-trained** evaluator causes more problems than no evaluator at all.
  The evaluator was **ill trained**.

  Management and the union finally agreed after months of **hard-nosed** negotiations.
  The negotiations were **hard nosed**.

Note: Some hyphenated adjectives, such as *old-fashioned* and *ladder-back,* and the words in the following section, keep their hyphens no matter where they are in a sentence. Check a recent dictionary when in doubt.

- Use a hyphen to join prefixes such as *self, half, ex, all, great, post, pro, former,* and *vice* or the suffix *elect* to words.

  The President unveiled the **all-powerful** orbiting space station.
  Lee Iacocca is a **self-made** man.
  You need to keep your **half-baked** plans a secret.
  Bobby saw his **ex-wife** leaving the drug store.
  Max's **great-grandfather** passed away on Wednesday.
  Senior citizens remember the **post-war** years with great fondness.
  The **treasurer-elect** picked up all the records from the presiding treasurer.

- Use a hyphen to avoid confusing or awkward spellings.

  The committee's job was to re-pair [not *repair*]the tournament participants.
  My mother decided to re-cover [not *recover*] her old rocking chair.
  The doorway had a bell-like [not *belllike*] shape.
  The accountant re-examined [not *reexamined*] the final totals.

- Use a hyphen to join a capital letter to a word.

  After that you'll see a T-intersection.
  Turn right at the first road after the S-curve.
  The carpenter used a T-square.

- Use a hyphen to write two-word numbers between 21 and 99 as words.

  seventy-two
  thirty-four
  ninety-nine

- Use a hyphen to join fractions written as words.

  one-half
  three-fourths

- Use a hyphen to join numbers to words used as a single adjective.

  four-year loan
  six-foot window
  seven-year lease
  two-year-old girl

Note: When a series of similar number-word adjectives is written in a sentence, use a hyphen/comma combination with all but the last item in the series.

Plywood comes in **two-, four-,** and **six-foot** sheets.
Joe scored three touchdowns on **twelve-, sixteen-,** and **five-yard** carries.

- Use an en dash to join numbers indicating a life span, a score, or the duration of an event.

  William Shakespeare (1564–1616) is the most widely read English writer.
  The Cyclones won the game 78–67.
  The speech should last 5–7 minutes.

- Use a hyphen to separate a word between syllables at the end of a line. Here are a few guidelines for dividing words:

  Never leave a single-letter syllable on a line.
  Divide hyphenated words at the hyphen.
  Never divide a one-syllable word.
  Avoid dividing words that have fewer than six letters.
  Avoid dividing the last word of a paragraph.
  Avoid dividing a number.
  When in doubt, always check a dictionary.

Practice

Add hyphens where they are needed in the following sentences. Check your work with the answers at the end of the chapter.

1. After examining your brain X rays, I see little justification for you to act like a know it all.
2. Linda May, now an ex corporate lawyer, reevaluated her career goals and became a self help author.
3. Eileen's well researched presentation impressed the audience of twenty five.
4. Allison's time in the one hundred meter dash beat mine by three tenths of a second.
5. After a day long business venture involving a water stand, the seven year old twins had made a ten cent profit.

PARENTHESES

- Use parentheses to enclose explanations that interrupt the normal flow of the sentence and are only marginally related to the text. Note: Parentheses are often interchangeable with dashes in this kind of sentence (see Chapter 10).

  Center Street (a party neighborhood if there ever was one) is a great place to live.
  The neighbors had a picnic on Fourth of July. (Fortunately, we were invited.)
  Unfortunately, another set of neighbors (they were not invited) called the police to complain about the noise (probably that of the illegal fireworks).
  We party-goers (how were we to know?) were completely surprised by the officers.

Notice the last three sentences. Each set of parentheses contains a complete sentence. If the parenthetical construction comes at the end of a sentence, it is punctuated as its own sentence within the parentheses. On the other hand, if it comes within another sentence, no capital letters or periods are necessary. However, if the parenthetical construction in the middle of another sentence is a sentence that would normally require a question mark or exclamation point, include that punctuation.

- Use parentheses to enclose information when accuracy is essential.

 The twin children of the deceased couple (Alma and Otto Priggi) requested an autopsy.
 The client agrees to pay the sum of two hundred twenty-five dollars ($225) per hour.

DIAGONAL MARK

Much like the hyphen, a **diagonal mark** (also called a **solidus** or a **slant mark**) is used to join words or numbers. The most frequent use of the diagonal is with the words *and/or*, which shows that the sentence refers to one or both of the words being joined.

 The cast will consent to interviews on radio and/or TV.
 Applesauce and/or blended fruits can replace oil in most cake recipes.

- Use a diagonal mark to separate numbers in a fraction.

 It takes us $4\frac{1}{2}$ hours to do the inventory at the end of the week.
 He'll want a $1\frac{5}{8}$-inch wrench for this nut.

NUMBERS

In newspaper writing, figures, or numerals, are used instead of words because they are easier to identify and read. However, a number at the beginning of a sentence is always written as a word. In more formal writing, follow these rules.

- If a number can be written as one or two words, write it as a word. Otherwise, write the numeral.

 We saw fifteen safety movies last year.

We saw 115 safety movies last year.
The student wrote "I will not talk in class" three hundred times.
The student wrote "I will not talk in class" 350 times.

- Use Arabic numerals (1, 2, 25) rather than Roman numerals (I, II, XXV).

- Always write a number at the beginning of sentence as a word even if it is more than two words.

One hundred twenty-five employees received year-end bonuses.

Practice

Use what you have learned about punctuation and capitalization to correct the following sentences. Check your work with the answers at the end of the chapter.

6. our new four wheel drive vehicle I have never liked Jeeps is in the shop again
7. sugar ray leonard what kind of name is sugar fought his way out of retirement several times
8. on delivery the recipient will pay the agreed on fee $435.67
9. employees bonuses will be time and or money for two fifths of our staff
10. 4 of the workers who received pink slips will be re evaluated

Answers

1. After examining your brain X-rays, I see little justification for you to act like a know-it-all.
2. Linda May, now an ex-corporate lawyer, re-evaluated her career goals and became a self-help author.
3. Eileen's well-researched presentation impressed the audience of twenty-five.
4. Allison's time in the one-hundred-meter dash beat mine by three-tenths of a second.
5. After a day-long business venture involving a water stand, the seven-year-old twins had made a ten-cent profit.
6. Our new four-wheel-drive vehicle (I have never liked Jeeps) is in the shop again.
7. Sugar Ray Leonard (what kind of name is "Sugar"?) fought his way out of retirement several times.
8. On delivery, the recipient will pay the agreed-on fee ($435.67).
9. Employees' bonuses will be time and/or money for two-fifths of our staff.
10. Four of the workers who received pink slips will be re-evaluated.

CHAPTER 12 GRAMMAR IQ QUIZ

Complete each sentence with the correct past-tense form of the verb listed. Answers and explanations follow the quiz.

1. cook When we arrived, he was ________dinner for us.
2. watch I ________ my niece while my sister went shopping.
3. open She ________ her own business in 2004, and it is thriving.
4. bake My mother ________ my favorite dish for my birthday last year.
5. show She ________ a different side to her personality during the meeting.
6. use My parents ________ to drink a lot of coffee.
7. Karen should (of, have) told me sooner.

Answers

1. cooking (present participle)
2. watched (past)
3. opened (past)
4. baked (past)
5. showed (past)
6. used (past)
7. Karen should **have** told me sooner

CHAPTER 12 VERBS THAT FOLLOW THE RULES

Verbs—words that show action or a state of being—drive written language and give it life. Because verbs are so important, mistakes involving verbs can be glaring. This chapter explains how to use verbs correctly in sentences.

Grammar concepts to know:

- **principal parts of verbs**—four basic forms of a verb
- **present**—principal part of a verb that describes action happening now—or routine action
- **present participle**—principal part of a verb that describes ongoing action and ends in *-ing*
- **past**—principal part of a verb that describes action that happened in the past
- **past participle**—principal part of a verb that describes action that happened in the past and is used with a helping verb, such as *has*, *have*, or *had*

Writers use words to communicate. Few things are more confusing to the reader than misusing words—especially verbs. Incorrect verb forms call special attention to themselves. This lesson explains how to use regular verbs correctly and highlights a few of the most common mistakes writers make.

Read the paragraph on the following page. This letter contains several errors in verb tense. Can you spot them? By the end of this chapter, you'll probably be able to correct them all.

Ben had an accident today. He and I were haul a load of furniture from the warehouse. As we drove, the end gate snap open and a box was fall out. Ben yell and I stoped. He putted it back in and slam the end gate shut. He snag his thumb in the latch. I looked at it and rubed it. I ask if he was hurt and would of taken him to the clinic. He seem okay, but later we learn his thumb was broken.

THE PRINCIPAL PARTS OF VERBS

Verbs have four principal parts, or fundamental forms that are used to create a tense: present, present participle, past, and past participle.

- **Present:** This refers to something that is existing or happening now, or to an action that happens routinely.

  I **walk** my dog every day.
  Thomas **is** here already.
  As soon as my mom **wakes** up, she **goes** straight into the kitchen to make a pot of coffee.

- **Present participle:** This is formed by adding *-ing* to the end of regular verbs. It is used with forms of the verb *to be*, such as *am*, *is*, *are*, *was*, or *were*. The present participle form of a verb expresses an ongoing action. (The helping verbs are used with the present participle determine tense, which is covered in Chapter 14.)

  I **am looking** for the notebook I lost in yesterday's class.
  I **was eating** dinner when she called.
  They **were trying** to decide where to go on vacation when I arrived.

- **Past:** This form of a verb is used to indicate that something has already been completed.

  I **hired** my assistant because his resume was impeccable.
  He **learned** Japanese during his semester abroad in Tokyo.
  They **placed** their trust in the new counselor.

- **Past participle:** This is formed by adding *-d* or *-ed* to the end of regular verbs. It is used with the helping verb *have* (*has, have,* or *had*). I **have learned** a thing or two in my life.

  She **has noticed** his weight gain.
  They already **had elected** a new chairwoman when she arrived.

REGULAR VERBS

Regular verbs follow a standard set of rules for forming their present participle and past forms. The present participle is formed by adding *-ing*. If the verb ends with the letter *e*, drop the *e* before adding *-ing*. The past is formed by adding *-ed*. If the verb ends with the letter *e*, just add *d*.

link: present form
linking: forms the present participle by adding *-ing*
linked: forms the past and past participle by adding *-ed*

prepare: present form
preparing: forms the present participle by dropping the *e* and adding *-ing*.
prepared: forms the past and past participle by adding *d*.

Here is a list of twenty regular verbs and all of their principal parts.

Present	Present Participle	Past	Past Participle
connect	connecting	connected	connected
elect	electing	elected	elected
exercise	exercising	exercised	exercised
follow	following	followed	followed
guarantee	guaranteeing	guaranteed	guaranteed
hire	hiring	hired	hired
imagine	imagining	imagined	imagined
knock	knocked	knocking	knocked
learn	learning	learned	learned
match	matching	matched	matched
notice	noticing	noticed	noticed
progress	progressing	progressed	progressed
rate	rating	rated	rated
salt	salting	salted	salted
solve	solving	solved	solved
target	targeting	targeted	targeted
time	timing	timed	timed
view	viewing	viewed	viewed
wash	washing	washed	washed
yell	yelling	yelled	yelled

Practice

Fill in the correct form of the verb in each of the following sentences. The present form of the verb comes at the beginning of each sentence. Check your work with the answers at the end of the chapter.

1. define — Paul __________ the word *impetus* for us.
2. leak — Water is __________ through the roof.
3. melt — The snow __________ early this year.
4. organize — Kay and Sandy are __________ the retirement dinner this year.
5. place — The custodian __________ an air freshener in the lounge.

REGULAR VERBS ENDING WITH A VOWEL AND CONSONANT

The English language has two kinds of letters: vowels and consonants. The vowels are *a, e, i, o, u*. All other letters are consonants. The letter *y*, however, sometimes works as a vowel and sometimes as a consonant.

When a verb ends with a vowel followed by a consonant (*blot, flip, occur*), the last consonant is doubled before adding *-ing* or *-ed*. The next table shows ten words that end this way. Look carefully at how the present participle and past forms are made.

net: present form
netting: forms the present participle by doubling the *t* before adding *-ing*
netted: forms the past and past participle by doubling the *t* and adding *-ed*

trip: present form
tripping: forms the present participle by doubling the *p* before adding *-ing*
tripped: forms the past and past participle by doubling the *p* and adding *-ed*

Present	Present Participle	Past	Past Participle
cap	capping	capped	capped
dab	dabbing	dabbed	dabbed
grab	grabbing	grabbed	grabbed
emit	emitting	emitted	emitted
occur	occurring	occurred	occurred
pin	pinning	pinned	pinned
scar	scarring	scarred	scarred
ship	shipping	shipped	shipped
step	stepping	stepped	stepped
trap	trapping	trapped	trapped

This rule has one exception. If the final consonant is a *w*, it is not doubled before adding *-ing* or *-ed*. Look at the following examples.

show: present form
showing: present participle
showed: past and past participle

sew: present form
sewing: present participle
sewed: past and past participle

Practice

Fill in the correct form of the verb in each of the following sentences. The present form of the verb comes at the beginning of each sentence. Check your work with the answers at the end of the chapter.

6. fit	My new shoes __________ my feet just fine.
7. map	The survey crew is __________ the plot this afternoon.
8. slow	Lyle __________ down as he approached the stop sign.
9. refer	I think he is __________ to the article in this morning's paper.
10. transfer	Marcia and Peg have __________ to the new location.

REGULAR VERBS ENDING WITH A CONSONANT FOLLOWED BY *Y*

When a verb ends with a consonant followed by *y* (*cry, empty, hurry*), the present participle is formed by adding *-ing*. To create the past form, drop the *y*, replace it with *i*, and add *-ed*. The examples show how this is done. The table that follows contains ten words that end in this way. Look carefully at how the past and past participles are formed.

fry: present form
frying: present participle
fried: forms the past and past participle by changing the *y* to *i* and adding *-ed*

study: present form
studying: present participle
studied: forms the past and past participle by changing the *y* to *i* and adding *-ed*

Present	Present Participle	Past	Past Participle
falsify	falsifying	falsified	falsified
magnify	magnifyin	magnified	magnified
marry	marrying	married	married
multiply	multiplying	multiplied	multiplied
occupy	occupying	occupied	occupied
pity	pitying	pitied	pitied
pry	prying	pried	pried
qualify	qualifying	qualified	qualified
unify	unifying	unified	unified
verify	verifying	verified	verified

Practice

Fill in the correct form of the verb in each of the following sentences. The present form of the verb comes at the beginning of each sentence. Check your work with the answers at the end of the chapter.

11. try The wolf __________ desperately to escape from the trap.
12. nullify The new contract __________ the old one.
13. tally The election committee is __________ the votes right now.
14. pity The children __________ the caged puppy.
15. qualify Marge's time in the race __________ her for the national meet.

ONE-PART REGULAR VERBS

Some verbs in the English language have the same present, past, and past participle form. The only time these verbs change is when *-ing* is added to form the present participle. Here is a partial list of those verbs, followed by several examples.

bet *hit* *set*
bid *hurt* *shut*
burst *put* *spread*
cost *quit* *upset*
cut *read*

The first baseman *hit* a home run. (present)
In yesterday's game, the first baseman *hit* a home run. (past)
The first baseman has *hit* twenty home runs so far this year. (past participle)
The first baseman is *hitting* yet another home run. (present participle—the only one that changes)

Don't Forget the *-ed*

Some words are written incorrectly because we don't always use or hear the *-ed* in spoken English. Remember to add *-ed* to the past and past participle forms of these words. The ones most commonly misused are shown in the next table.

Present	Present Participle	Past	Past Participle
ask	asking	asked	asked
risk	risking	risked	risked
suppose	supposing	supposed	supposed
use	using	used	used

We asked [not *ask*] to see the record book.
The rescuers risked [not *risk*] their lives to save the stranded mountain climbers.
We are supposed [not *suppose*] to finish this for tomorrow.
This group is used [not *use*] to working together.

Don't Use *of* in Place of *have*

Another problem resulting from pronunciation is using *of* instead of *have* in participial phrases. *Could've* sounds just like *could of*—but *could have* is correct and *could of* is wrong.

Wrong: Hansel could **of** seen the danger if he had looked more carefully.
Correct: Hansel could **have** seen the danger if he had looked more carefully.

Wrong: The farmer should **of** warned us about the dog.
Correct: The farmer should **have** warned us about the dog.

Wrong: I wish the contractor would **of** taken care of this for us.
Correct: I wish the contractor would **have** taken care of this for us.

Practice

Use what you have learned about verbs to correct the following sentences. Check your work with the corrected sentences that follow.

16. Sally wish her husband would of remembered to pack her lunch.
17. That's not the way we use to do it.
18. Juwon risk serious injury by wipe the acid spill.
19. You could of improved your chances by preparing ahead of time.
20. Ryan ask the question that the rest of us were afraid to ask.

REVIEW

Remember the paragraph at the beginning of the chapter? Take another look at it and correct all of the errors you find. Compare your version to the corrected version below. The changes have been bolded for you.

> Ben had an accident today. He and I were haul**ing** a load of furniture from the warehouse. As we drove, the end gate snap**p**ed open and a box **fell** out. Ben yell**ed** and I stop**p**ed. He **put** it back in and slam**m**ed the end gate shut. He snag**ged** his thumb in the latch. I looked at it and rub**b**ed it. I asked if he was hurt and would **have** taken him to the clinic. He seem**ed** okay, but later**,** we learn**ed** his thumb was broken.

Answers

1. defined
2. leaking
3. melted
4. organizing
5. placed
6. fit
7. mapping
8. slowed
9. referring
10. transferred
11. tried
12. nullified (or nullifies)
13. tallying
14. pitied

15. qualified
16. Sally wished her husband would have remembered to pack her lunch.
17. That's not the way we used to do it.
18. Juwon risked serious injury by wiping the acid spill.
19. You could have improved your chances by preparing ahead of time.
20. Ryan asked the question that the rest of us were afraid to ask.

CHAPTER 13 GRAMMAR IQ QUIZ

Choose the correct form of the verb in each of the following sentences. Answers follow the quiz.

1. The teacher (ask, asked) the student a question.
2. Life (dealed, dealt) me a good hand.
3. The plumbers (do, did, done) a good job of stopping the leak.
4. The lake will (freeze, froze, frozen) over by morning.
5. My new diet has not yet (begin, began, begun) to work.

Answers

1. asked
2. dealt
3. did
4. freeze
5. begun

REBELLIOUS VERBS

The last chapter explained how and when to use regular verbs. This chapter explains how to use irregular verbs—the ones that don't follow the rules.

Grammar concept to know:

- **irregular verb**—a verb that forms its past and past participle forms in a unique way

Most verbs in the English language are regular, but approximately 150 verbs are not. Most of the irregularities involve the ways in which the past and past participle are formed. This chapter covers many of these verbs and provides practice in using them. Read the following note, written by an employee to a supervisor. How many errors in using irregular verbs can you spot?

> I done what you ask this morning. I digged through the recycling bin to look for your records. I seen a few things that seemed like what we was looking for, but I think last night's trash must have went to the dumpster, and I ain't digging in there.

IRREGULAR VERBS WITH SIMILAR PAST AND PAST PARTICIPLE FORMS

This table includes some of the most commonly used irregular verbs. All of them have the same past and past participle, except for the last three. The last three words form their principal parts in the same way and have a past participle form that is similar, though not identical, to the past form. Following the table are some exercises in using these verbs.

Present	**Past**	**Past Participle (used with *have, has, had*)**
bite	bit	bit
dig	dug	dug
bleed	bled	bled
hear	heard	heard
hold	held	held
light	lit	lit
meet	met	met
pay	paid	paid
say	said	said
sell	sold	sold
tell	told	told
shine	shone	shone
shoot	shot	shot
sit	sat	sat
spin	spun	spun
spit	spat	spat
win	won	won
swear	swore	sworn
tear	tore	torn
wear	wore	worn

Practice

Choose the correct form of the verb in each of the sentences that follow. Remember to use present tense for things happening now, and past tense for things that have already happened. Check your work with the answers at the end of the chapter.

1. The dentist (ask, asked) me to (bite, bit) down hard on the X-ray tabs.
2. Dark-colored garments (bleed, bled) freely in hot water.

3. I (hear, heard) yesterday that you plan to move before summer.
4. Will (pay, paid) his bills with a credit card.
5. It's cold enough to (light, lit) the furnace.
6. Breanna never (tell, told) us what you meant.
7. The moon (shine, shone) through the trees, making eerie shadows on the ground.
8. The tires did nothing but (spin, spun) on the glare ice.
9. If we (win, won) this game, we advance to the playoffs.
10. Collin (tear, tore) his jeans climbing over the barbed wire fence.

MORE IRREGULAR VERBS WITH TWO IDENTICAL PARTS

Here's another table of irregular verbs whose past and past participle are the same. Study them, and then complete the exercises that follow.

Present	Past	Past Participle (used with have, has, had)
creep	crept	crept
deal	dealt	dealt
keep	kept	kept
kneel	knelt	knelt
leave	left	left
mean	meant	meant
send	sent	sent
sleep	slept	slept
spend	spent	spent
sweep	swept	swept
bring	brought	brought
buy	bought	bought
catch	caught	caught
fight	fought	fought
teach	taught	taught
think	thought	thought
feed	fed	fed
flee	fled	fled
find	found	found
grind	ground	ground

Practice

Choose the correct form of the verb in each of the following sentences. Remember to use present tense for things happening now, and past tense for things that have already happened. Check your work with the answers at the end of the chapter.

11. The gambler folded the hand he was (deal, dealt).
12. The detectives (keep, kept) the suspect under surveillance all last night.
13. The would-be knight (kneel, knelt) before the king.
14. Do you (mean, meant) that we'll be without electricity all evening?
15. The twins (spend, spent) last evening with their grandparents.
16. We always (bring, brought) deviled eggs to every family picnic.
17. The centerfielder (catch, caught) the ball and threw it to home plate.
18. Hal (think, thought) the fruit would have been delivered by now.
19. We (find, found) water in our basement every spring.
20. The deer (flee, fled) after they saw our headlights.

IRREGULAR VERBS WITH THREE DISTINCT FORMS

The irregular verbs in this table are grouped with other verbs that form their principal parts in similar ways. See if you can detect any patterns or groups in these irregular verbs.

Present	Past	Past Participle (used with have, has, had)
begin	began	begun
ring	rang	rung
sing	sang	sung
spring	sprang	sprung
do	did	done
go	went	gone
am	was	been
is	was	been
drink	drank	drunk
shrink	shrank	shrunk
sink	sank	sunk
stink	stank	stunk
blow	blew	blown
draw	drew	drawn
grow	grew	grown

Present	Past	Past Participle (used with *have, has, had*)
know	knew	known
throw	threw	thrown
fly	flew	flown
drive	drove	driven
strive	strove	striven

Practice

Choose the correct form of the verb in each of the following sentences. Remember to use present tense for things happening now, past tense for things that have already happened, and past participle with *have, has,* or *had.* Check your work with the answers at the end of the chapter.

21. It has (begin, began, begun) to rain.
22. The congregation (sing, sang, sung) the first two verses of the hymn.
23. The builder (do, did, done) all the planning for us.
24. The neighbors have (go, went, gone) on vacation.
25. Jack (is, was, has been) putting in overtime for that last three weeks.
26. The sweatshirt (shrink, shrank, shrunk) when I washed it.
27. The ship must have (sink, sank, sunk) about 125 years ago.
28. All of their children have (grow, grew, grown) up and moved away.
29. The proprietor (know, knew, known) his supplies were running short.
30. The teenage boy (drive, drove, driven) his way to high insurance rates.

MORE THREE-PART IRREGULAR VERBS

The next table also includes verbs grouped with others that form their principal parts in similar ways. See if you can detect the patterns.

Present	Past	Past Participle (used with *have, has, had*)
choose	chose	chosen
rise	rose	risen
break	broke	broken
speak	spoke	spoken
fall	fell	fallen
shake	shook	shaken
take	took	taken
forget	forgot	forgotten

Present	**Past**	**Past Participle (used with *have, has, had*)**
get	got	gotten
give	gave	given
forgive	forgave	forgiven
forsake	forsook	forsaken
hide	hid	hidden
ride	rode	ridden
write	wrote	written
come	came	come
overcome	overcame	overcome
run	ran	run
freeze	froze	frozen
steal	stole	stolen

Practice

Choose the correct form of the verb in each of the sentences that follow. Remember to use present tense for things happening now, past tense for things that have already happened, and past participle with *have, has,* or *had.* Check your work with the answers at the end of the chapter.

31. The gambler must have (choose, chose, chosen) the lucky dice.
32. The band on this watch (break, broke, broken).
33. Hoards of walnuts (fall, fell, fallen) from the tree that fall.
34. The audience grew deathly quiet when they realized the star had (forget, forgot, forgotten) his lines.
35. Becky's parents (give, gave, given) her clothes for Christmas.
36. The dog must have (hide, hid, hidden) your slippers.
37. Have you (write, wrote, written) to your mother lately?
38. The newlyweds (come, came) home to a completely empty house.
39. Water will (freeze, froze, frozen) at 32 degrees Fahrenheit.
40. More time has been (steal, stole, stolen) by procrastination than any other thief.

Ain't

Ain't is a substandard English word that should never be used in business language. It belongs in the same category as *wanna* and *gonna*. You may hear these words when people speak, but they are not used in formal writing. Instead of *ain't*, use *is not* or *isn't*, *am not*, and *are not* or *aren't*.

Incorrect: I ain't interested in your product.
Correct: I am not interested in your product.

Incorrect: He ain't the problem here.
Correct: He isn't the problem here.

Incorrect: We ain't supposed to know about the party.
Correct: We aren't supposed to know about the party.

REVIEW

Remember the paragraph at the beginning of the chapter? Take another look at it and correct all of the verb errors you find. Compare your version of the paragraph to the corrected one that follows. The changes have been bolded for you.

> I **did** what you asked this morning. I **dug** through the recycling bin to look for your records. I **saw** a few things that seemed like what we **were** looking for, but I think last night's trash must have **gone** to the dumpster, and I'**m not** digging in there.

Practice

Choose the correct form of the verb in each of the following sentences. Check your work with the answers at the end of the chapter.

41. Your department certainly (do, did, done) a good job on this project.
42. The manager just (throw, threw, thrown) away a chance to increase the store's sales.
43. The president (speak, spoke, spoken) at the cabinet meeting.
44. The phone has (ring, rang, rung) continuously all day long.
45. The minister (come, came) to the point very early in the sermon.

46. Harriet (see, saw, seen) the advertisement for the new product in a catalog.
47. The new tree has not yet (begin, began, begun) to produce fruit.
48. Has the admitting staff (go, went, gone) nuts?
49. Heather lost a filling when she (bite, bit, bitten) into the piece of hard candy.
50. The attendant couldn't believe that someone had actually (steal, stole, stolen) a car from the ramp.

Answers

1. asked, bite
2. bleed
3. heard
4. paid
5. light
6. told
7. shone
8. spin
9. win
10. tore
11. dealt
12. kept
13. knelt
14. mean
15. spent
16. bring
17. caught
18. thought
19. find
20. fled
21. begun
22. sang
23. did
24. gone
25. has been
26. shrank
27. sunk
28. grown
29. knew
30. drove
31. chosen
32. broke
33. fell
34. forgotten
35. gave
36. hidden
37. written
38. came
39. freeze
40. stolen
41. did
42. threw
43. spoke
44. rung
45. came
46. saw
47. begun
48. gone
49. bit
50. stolen

CHAPTER 14 GRAMMAR IQ QUIZ

Choose the correct verb form in each of the following sentences. Answers follow the quiz.

1. Hilary (realize, realized, had realized) that she (leave, left, had left) her purse inside the house.
2. The representative (think, thought, had thought) the merchandise (ship, shipped, had been shipped) the day before.
3. Miguel (knocks, knocked, had knocked) and (rings, rang, had rung) the doorbell.
4. Since the supplies (arrive, arrived, had arrived), we (begin, began, had begun) to work.
5. The new superintendent (is, was, been) very friendly. [Assume that the superintendent is living.]

Answers

1. realized, had left
2. thought, had been shipped
3. knocked, rang *or* knocks, rings *or* had knocked, had rung
4. had arrived, began
5. is

DON'T BE TENSE ABOUT VERBS

Yesterday, today, and tomorrow: This chapter covers the fine points of verb tenses, the verb forms that express the time an action occurs. By the end of this chapter you'll have a better understanding of how to use past-, present-, and future-tense verbs.

Grammar concepts to know:

- **verb tense**—form of a verb that indicates when the action occurs
- **subjunctive mood**—form of a verb used to indicate a condition contrary to fact

Verb tense tells readers the time an action takes place, so writers need to know how to use it accurately. This chapter explains how to keep verb tense consistent and when to switch tense.

KEEPING VERB TENSE CONSISTENT

The tense of a verb tells when an action occurs, occurred, or will occur. Verbs have three basic tenses: present, past, and future. A passage that begins in present tense should continue in present tense. If it begins in past tense, it should stay in past tense. Do not mix tenses as you write.

Wrong: The officer **unlocked** the trunk and **searches** for contraband.
Correct: The officer **unlocked** the trunk and **searched** for contraband.
Correct: The officer **unlocks** the trunk and **searches** for contraband.

Wrong: When we **increase** advertising expenses, we **reduced** profits.
Correct: When we **increase** advertising expenses, we **reduce** profits.
Correct: When we **increased** advertising expenses, we **reduced** profits.

USING TENSE TO CONVEY MEANING

Using verb tense carefully helps writers avoid confusing the reader. The following examples illustrate how tense can completely change the meaning of a sentence.

Richard discovered that Patty had left home and gone to work. (Patty had gone to work.)
Richard discovered that Patty had left home and went to work. (Richard went to work.)

Linda already had bought groceries and cooked dinner when Hal arrived. (When Hal arrived, Linda had already completed two actions before his arrival—she had bought groceries and cooked dinner.)
Linda already had bought groceries and was cooking dinner when Hal arrived. (When Hal arrived, Linda had completed one action—she had bought groceries—and was in the middle of another action-cooking dinner.)

THE FINE POINTS OF VERB TENSE

Sometimes, a writer must show that an action occurred at another time, regardless of the tense in which the passage begins. To allow this, each of the three basic tenses has three subdivisions: progressive, perfect, and progressive perfect.

Present tense shows action that happens now or action that happens routinely. The **present progressive** tense shows an action that is happening now. A helping, or auxiliary, verb (*am, is,* or *are*) always precedes the *-ing* form (progressive form) of the verb to create the present progressive tense. The **present perfect** tense shows an action that was completed in the indefinite past. A helping verb (*have* or *has*) precedes the past form of the verb to create this tense. The **present perfect progressive** tense shows action that began in the past and is continuing in the present to create this tense, helping verbs (*have been* or *has been*) precede the verb written in its *-ing* form (progressive form).

Present	**Present Progressive**	**Present Perfect**	**Present Perfect Progressive**
(shows action happening now or routinely)	(*-ing* form preceded by *am, is, are*)	(shows action that began in the past; uses *has, have*)	(shows action that began in the past and continues now; uses *has* or *have been*)
Optimists hope for the best. Smoking causes cancer in millions of people.	Optimists are hoping for the best. Smoking is causing cancer in millions of people.	Optimists have hoped for the best. Smoking has caused cancer in millions of people.	Optimists have been hoping for the best. Smoking has been causing cancer in millions of people.

All present-tense forms can be used without shifting verb tense. Read the paragraph below to see how this is done. The verbs are italicized, and the words in parentheses identify the tense.

> The city planners *are hoping* (present progressive) to revamp the old stadium, which the Redbirds *use* (present). For years fans *have complained* (present perfect) about parking, and officials *pay* (present) little attention. Season ticket holders *have been boycotting* (present perfect progressive) games for the last month, but their absence *has gone* (present perfect) unnoticed. They *demand* (present) adequate parking.

Past tense shows action that was completed in the past. It uses the past form of the verb. The **past progressive** tense shows an ongoing action in the past. To form this tense, a helping verb (*was* or *were*) precedes the progressive form of the verb. The **past perfect** tense shows an action completed in the past before some other past action. The helping verb *had* precedes the past participle form of the verb to form the past perfect. The **past perfect progressive** tense shows continuing action that began in the past before another action in the past. The helping verbs *had been* precede the progressive form of the verb to form this tense.

Past	Past Progressive	Past Perfect	Past Perfect Progressive
(action completed in the past)	(*-ing* form, continuing action in the past; uses *was, were*)	(action completed prior to another action; uses *had*)	(continuing action in the past before another action in the past; uses *had been*)
Parents spoke to the teachers.	Parents were speaking to the teachers.	Parents had already spoken to the teachers.	Parents had been speaking to the teachers for half an hour by the time I arrived.
The principal held the meetings.	The principal was holding the meetings.	The principal had already held the meetings.	The principal had been holding the meetings before the math teacher took over.

All past-tense forms can be used in one writing passage, as they do not constitute a shift in tense. The paragraph that follows illustrates how this is done. The verbs are italicized, and the words in parentheses identify the tense.

> Last fall, school officials *warned* (past) students about bringing cell phones to school. Most students *complied* (past) with the request; however, some *ignored* (past) the rules and *continued* (past) to carry the cells they *had been bringing* (past perfect progressive) to school. They *had carried* (past perfect) them the previous year and *planned* (past) to continue. Around mid-year, several students *were suspended* (past). A *Times* reporter, who *had been following* (past perfect progressive) the story, *challenged* (past) the legality of the school's rule. A suit *has been filed* (past perfect) on behalf of the suspended students, but it *has* not *come* (past perfect) before the court.

Future tense shows action that has yet to happen. The helping verbs *will, would,* or *shall* precede the present form of the verb to form the future tense. The **future progressive** tense shows ongoing actions in the future. To form this tense, the helping-verb phrases *will be, shall be,* or *would be* precede the progressive form of the verb. The **future perfect** tense shows actions that will be completed. The helping-verb phrases *will have, would have,* or *will have been* precede the past participle form of the verb to form the future perfect. The **future perfect progressive** tense shows continuing actions that will be completed before another future action or time. The verb phrases *will have been*, *would have been*, or *shall have been* precede the progressive form of the verb to form this tense.

Future	Future Progressive	Future Perfect	Future Perfect Progressive
(action that will happen; uses *will*, *would*, *shall*)	(continuing action that will happen)	(action that will be completed before another future action or time)	(continuing action that will be completed before another future action or time)
We will begin a letter-writing campaign.	Everyone will be writing letters.	By summer, we will have written reams of letters.	By then, legislaters will have been receiving letters throughout the year.
Newspapers will cover this case.	Newspapers will be covering this case.	By summer, every newspaper will have written about this case.	By summer, newspapers will have been covering the case for three months.

All future-tense forms can be used in one writing passage, as they do not constitute a shift in tense. The next paragraph illustrates how this is done. The verbs are italicized and the words in parentheses identify the tense.

> Because so many people are moving to the area, K & M Real Estate **will develop** (future) the land just east of the river. This **will assure** (future) that the property value of the surrounding neighborhood **will increase** (future). K & M **will be building** (future progressive) modern condominiums, which will add a nice aesthetic to the neighborhood. By next spring, the park next to the condos **will have been completed** (future perfect), and people **will have been living** (future perfect progressive) in the condos since February.

IMPROPER USE OF PAST TENSE

Don't use past tense to make a statement about a present condition.

> Zelda met the new director. He **was** very tall. [Isn't he still tall?]
> Zelda met the new director. He **is** very tall.

I visited a bed and breakfast inn near the edge of town. The building **was** Victorian. [Isn't it still Victorian?]

I visited a bed and breakfast inn near the edge of town. The building **is** Victorian.

PRESENT TENSE FOR STATEMENTS OF GENERAL TRUTH OR FACT

Even if a passage is written in past tense, a general statement of truth or fact is written in present tense.

During Galileo's time, few people *believed* (past) that the earth *revolves* (present) around the sun.

The engineer *explained* (past) to the city council that the streets *run* (present) parallel to the freeway.

SUBJUNCTIVE MOOD FOR CONDITIONS CONTRARY TO FACT

When Tevya in *Fiddler on the Roof* sings, "If I were a rich man . . ." he uses the verb *were* to signal that he is only imagining what he would do as a rich man. The subjunctive mood of verbs is used to express something that is wished for or that is contrary to fact. The subjunctive of *was* is *were.*

If you *were* a cat, you would be entirely dependent on human beings. [You are not a cat.]

If Anthony *were* more responsible, he could be trusted with this job. [Anthony is not responsible.]

Practice

Use what you have learned about verb tense to choose the correct option in each of the following sentences. Check your work with the answers on the following page.

1. After Ethel knocked on the door, she (ring, rang, had rung) the doorbell.
2. By the time I get on the plane, she will (read, have read) my love letter.
3. My teacher explained why Mars (is, was) red.
4. I would finish the job if I (was, were) you.
5. The office morale has already (begin, began, begun) to suffer.

6. Yesterday, the nurse (takes, took) my pulse and (measures, measured) my blood pressure.
7. Most of us wish we would (of, have) taken stock options rather than year-end bonuses.
8. Charles wishes he had ordered a large burger because his (is, was) too small.
9. Dr. Carnes announced that the department chair (is, was) responsible for work schedules.
10. The packing plant could cut transportation costs if it (was, were) closer to a livestock confinement.
11. After I rented the movie, I realized that I already (saw, had seen, have seen) it.
12. If I (was, were) president of the United States, I'd abolish income taxes.
13. Alvin opened the door and (look, looks, looked) inside.
14. When we increase maintenance service, we (reduce, reduced) repair costs.
15. The company had dumped waste into the river for years and it (plans, planned, had planned) to continue doing so until new laws were passed.
16. I met the new technician. He (is, was) very personable.
17. Because Peter loved his job, he (takes, took) it very seriously.
18. I ate at a new restaurant last night, and the decor (is, was) wonderful.
19. I like knowing that my work (is, was) done well.
20. Hesari has been desperate to (take, took, have taken) time off work.

Answers

1. rang
2. have read
3. is
4. were
5. begun
6. took/measured
7. have
8. is
9. is
10. were
11. had seen
12. were
13. looked
14. reduce
15. planned
16. is
17. took
18. is
19. is
20. take

CHAPTER 15 GRAMMAR IQ QUIZ

Choose the verb that matches the subject in each of the following sentences. Answers follow the quiz.

1. The child (doesn't, don't) want to go to bed just yet.
2. One of the assignments (is, are) missing.
3. Aerobics (is, are) good for general health and weight management.
4. Either of these faucets (is, are) fine for the bathroom sink.
5. Either Eugene or Bernice (want, wants) to go on a week-long cruise.
6. There (isn't, aren't) many files left to read.
7. Neither the coach nor the players (knows, know) the score.
8. Neither the players nor the coach (knows, know) the score.
9. The manager, as well as the associates, (is, are) scheduled to work the late shift.
10. The package (wasn't, weren't) where we had left it.

Answers

1. doesn't (child doesn't…)
2. is (one assignment is…)
3. is (Aerobics is one type of activity.)
4. is (either faucet is…)
5. wants (Eugene wants, Bernice wants)
6. aren't (files aren't…)
7. know (players know...)
8. knows (coach knows...)
9. is (manager is...)
10. wasn't (package wasn't…)

MAKING SUBJECTS AND VERBS AGREE

He don't or he doesn't? Most native English speakers automatically choose the second version. Subject-verb agreement is so important in speaking and writing that errors in this area really stand out. This chapter highlights some of the situations that cause agreement problems even for native speakers and explains how to handle them correctly in writing.

Grammar concepts to know:

- **subject-verb agreement**—when a subject in a sentence matches the verb in number
- **compound subject**—two or more subjects that share the same verb and that are joined by a conjunction

When the subject of a clause—the person or thing doing the action—matches the verb in number (both singular or both plural), we say the subject and verb are *in agreement.* Most English speakers have little trouble matching subjects with the correct verbs, but a few grammatical constructions do pose some problems. This chapter explains the concept of subject-verb agreement and provides practice in problem areas.

The memo on the following page contains several subject-verb agreement errors. See how many you can spot. By the end of this chapter, you should be able to recognize them all.

To: Jessica Amerson
From: Tyson Hall
Re: Aides/floor nurse dispute
Date: July 21, 1997

The nurse's aides was having trouble with the floor nurse yesterday. He don't think he should help with unloading supplies. Every one of the aides are just as busy as he is. The aides think he should do his part too. They wasn't very happy with him when he refused. Melinda and Connie is thinking about filing a complaint. Neither the aides nor the floor nurse need this fuss. Maybe you can see if either the floor nurse or the aides is willing to find a better solution.

MAKING SUBJECTS AGREE WITH THEIR VERBS IN NUMBER

A subject should agree with its verb in number. In other words, if a subject is singular, the verb must be singular; if the subject is plural, the verb must be plural. If you are unsure whether a verb is singular or plural, apply this simple test. Fill in the blanks in the two sentences that follow with the matching form of the verb. The verb form that best completes the first sentence is singular. The verb form that best completes the second sentence is plural.

He ______. [singular]
They ______. [plural]

Look at these examples using the verbs *look*, *do*, and *was*. Try it yourself with any verb that confuses you. Unlike nouns, most verbs ending in *s* are singular.

He looks.	He does.	He was.	[singular]
They look.	They do.	They were.	[plural]

Note, however, that the subject *I*, even though it is a single person, usually takes the plural form.

I look. I do. I am.

Problem Verb Forms and Constructions

The verb form *to be—be, am, is, are, was, were*—can pose special problems because the principal parts are formed in such unusual ways. The following list shows how to use the verb form *to be.*

Subject	Present	Past	Past Participle
I	I am	I was	I have been
you	you are	you were	you have been
he, she, it	he is	she was	it has been
we	we are	we were	we have been
they	they are	they were	they have been

Never use the *be* form after a subject.

> **Incorrect:** I be going.
> **Correct:** I am going.
>
> **Incorrect:** They be on their way.
> **Correct:** They are on their way.

Two other constructions often cause problems for people: *doesn't/don't* (meaning *does not, do not*) and *wasn't/weren't* (meaning *was not, were not*). *Doesn't* and *wasn't* are singular; *don't* and *weren't* are plural. (But remember that *I* takes the plural form.)

> I don't want to move until next year.
> She doesn't want to move until next year.
> They don't want to move until next year.
>
> I wasn't sure.
> You weren't sure.
> We weren't sure.

Phrases Following Subjects Don't Affect Verbs

Pay careful attention to the subject in a sentence. Do not allow a phrase following it to mislead you into using a verb that does not agree with the subject. The subjects and verbs are in bold in the following examples.

> **One** of the chairs **is** damaged.
> The window **designs** by Rick Baker **are** complex and colorful.
> A **manual** with thorough instructions **comes** with this printer.
> The **principal**, along with her three associates, **returns** from the workshop today.

Special Singular Subjects

Some nouns are singular even though they end in *s*. Despite that they sound plural, they require a singular verb because we think of them as a single unit. Most of the nouns in the following list are singular. Some can be either singular or plural, depending on their use in the sentence. These are just a few examples: *measles, mumps, news, checkers* or *marbles* (games), *physics, economics, mathematics, civics, athletics, sports, politics, statistics.*

The **news is** over at 9:30.
Darts is my favorite game.
Sports is a healthy stress reliever. Low-impact **aerobics is** best for older adults.

Words that express an amount may be singular or plural. Amounts are singular when the amount is thought of as a unit, and plural when the amount is thought of as many parts.

Six dollars **is** the price of a hamburger at the Corner Bistro. [Six dollars is thought of as one unit.]
Six dollars **are** lying on the table. [The dollars are thought of separately.]

Three hours **was** a long time to wait for the bus. [one unit of time]
Three hours of each day **were** dedicated to studying. [separate times]

A fraction is singular when it refers to a singular word and plural when it refers to a plural word.

One-fourth of my time **is** spent at the gym. [The fraction refers to the singular noun time.]
One-fourth of the people **are** here for the cooking class. [The fraction refers to the plural noun people.]

Practice

Circle the correct verb in each of the following sentences. Answers are found at the end of the chapter.

1. When the boss (jokes, joke), we (laughs, laugh).
2. A single tree now (grows, grow) where the forest used to (grows, grow).
3. Constella (speaks, speak) English, but her parents (speaks, speak) Spanish.
4. The clerk (rings, ring) up the sales while the customers (waits, wait) in line.
5. The carolers (hums, hum) while the soloist (sings, sing).

6. The bright walls (doesn't, don't) seem very relaxing.
7. The shipment (wasn't, weren't) here when we arrived this morning.
8. The bank (doesn't, don't) open until 9:30 on Saturday mornings.
9. Mabel couldn't drive to work because her car (wasn't, weren't) starting.
10. Paula (doesn't, don't) think the files (is, are) in storage.
11. One of the secretaries (is, are) finishing the newsletter that (was, were) scheduled to go out last week.
12. The petty cash box, along with the receipts, (is, are) turned in at the end of the day.
13. These statistics (is, are) the result of careful research.
14. Statistics (was, were) my most difficult math course in high school.
15. Half of the sandwich (was, were) eaten.
16. Half of the sandwiches (was, were) tuna salad.

MAKING PRONOUN SUBJECTS MATCH THEIR VERBS IN NUMBER

A **pronoun** is a word that takes the place of a noun. For example, in this sentence, "All of the cookies were decorated," the word *all* stands for or refers to cookies, and acts as the subject.

Pronouns used as subjects present a problem for even the most sophisticated speakers of English. Some pronouns are always plural. Other pronouns are always singular. Some of these are also called **indefinite pronouns** because they refer to no specific person of thing. A handful of pronouns can be either singular or plural.

Singular Pronouns

These pronouns are always singular. They require singular verbs.

each	*anyone*	*nobody*
either	*everybody*	*one*
neither	*everyone*	*somebody*
anybody	*no one*	*someone*

See how these pronouns take singular verbs in the following examples:

Someone always **forgets** to sign in.
Neither child **wants** to miss the fireworks.
Each of the members **feels** that an increase in dues is justified.
Everybody here **thinks** the car should be fixed instead of traded in for a new model.

Each, either, and *neither* are the pronouns most commonly misused. You can avoid making mistakes when using these pronouns by mentally replacing the other words between the pronoun and the verb with the word *one*. Look at the following examples to see how this is done.

Each of the boys wants his own car.
Each *one* **wants** his own car.

Either of the associates knows where the records are kept.
Either *one* **knows** where the records are kept.

These sentences may sound awkward. So many speakers misuse these pronouns that you may have become accustomed to hearing them used incorrectly. Despite that, the substitution trick (*one* for the words following the pronoun) will help you avoid this mistake.

For questions beginning with *has* or *have*, remember that *has* is singular while *have* is plural. Pay special attention to the verb-subject combination in a question. In fact, the correct verb is easier to identify if you turn the question into a statement.

(Is, Are) some of the advertisers noticing the difference?
Some of the advertisers **are** noticing the difference.

(Has, Have) either of the inspectors filed a report?
Either *one* **has** filed a report.

(Does, Do) each of the trucks have a hoist?
Each *one* **does** have a hoist.

Plural Pronouns

These pronouns are always plural and require a plural verb:

both *many*
few *several*

Singular/Plural Pronouns

The following pronouns can be either singular or plural:

all *none*
any *some*
most

The words that these pronouns refer to determine whether the verbs are singular or plural. If the pronoun refers to a plural noun or pronoun, the verb must be plural. If the pronoun refers to a singular noun or pronoun, the verb must be singular. See how this is done in the following sentences. The key words are in bold.

Singular	Plural
All of the **work is** planned.	**All** of the **jobs are** planned.
Is any of the **pie** remaining?	**Are any** of the **pieces** of pie remaining?
Most of the **milk was** sour.	**Most** of the **glasses** of milk **were** empty.
None of the **time was** spent very well.	**None** of the **hours were** spent very well.
Some of the **fruit was** shipped.	**Some** of the **apples were** shipped.

Practice

Practice matching pronoun subjects with verbs by circling the correct verb in each of the following sentences. Answers are found at the end of the chapter.

17. None of these keys (unlocks, unlock) the back door.
18. Each of the project components (takes, take) several hours to complete.
19. All of the box lunches (has, have) been given away.
20. Some of the animals (was, were) moved for the winter.
21. Either of these paintings (is, are) perfect for my house.
22. (Was, Were) any of the cables long enough?
23. (Do, Does) each of the keyboards have a built-in wrist support?
24. (Has, Have) either of the tenants paid the rent?
25. Neither of our fleet vehicles (needs, need) to be serviced.
26. Both of the trainees (seems, seem) motivated.
27. A friend at one of my jobs also (works, work) for the city.
28. None of our problems (goes, go) unnoticed by the regular customers.
29. An exercise program (helps, help) your frame of mind.
30. Each of these decongestants (causes, cause) drowsiness.

COMPOUND SUBJECTS

A compound subject is made up of two or more subjects that are joined by a conjunction (usually *and, or*, or *nor*) and that share the same verb.

Singular Subjects Joined by *and*

If two singular nouns or pronouns are joined by *and*, they require a plural verb.

He and she [both] **want** to take a vacation.
Jack and Jill [both] **insist** on finding a flat prairie on which to walk.

Singular Subjects Joined by *or* or *nor*

If two singular nouns or pronouns are joined by *or* or *nor*, they require a singular verb. Think of them as two separate sentences and you'll never make a mistake in agreement.

Art or Elaine **wants** to get a new car.
Art **wants** to get a new car.
Elaine **wants** to get a new car.

Singular and Plural Subjects Joined by *or* or *nor*

Singular and plural subjects joined by *or* or *nor* require a verb that agrees with the subject closest to the verb.

Neither the coach nor the **players like** the lineup.
Neither the players nor the **coach likes** the lineup.

VERBS AGREE WITH SUBJECTS, NOT THE WORD FOLLOWING THE VERB

Take care not to let the words following the verb confuse you about the real subject of the sentence.

Taxes were the biggest issue in the campaign.
The biggest **issue** in the campaign **was** taxes.

A serious **problem** for corn growers **is** weeds.
Weeds are a serious problem for corn growers.

WHEN THE SUBJECT FOLLOWS THE VERB

When a sentence asks a question or begins with the word *there* or *here*, the subject follows the verb. Locate the subject of the sentence and make certain the verb matches it. In the following example sentences, the subjects and verbs are bolded in the correct sentences.

Wrong	Correct
What is the terms of the agreement?	What **are** the **terms** of the agreement?
Why is his words garbled?	Why **are** his **words** garbled?
Here's the statistics they compiled.	Here **are** the **statistics** they compiled.
There is six students asking for help.	There **are** six **students** asking for help.

Inverted sentences also contain a subject that follows, rather than precedes, a verb. Locate the subject in an inverted sentence and make certain the verb agrees with it. In the example sentences that follow, the subjects and verbs in the corrected sentences are bolded.

Wrong	Correct
Inside your drawer is the documents I finished.	Inside your drawer are the documents I finished.
Out of nowhere comes three new accounts.	Out of nowhere come three new accounts.
Up in the stands go the fan who spilled my drink.	Up in the stands goes the fan who spilled my drink.

Practice

Practice what you have learned about matching verbs and subjects by choosing the correct verb in each of the following sentences. Check your work with the answers on the following page.

31. Every other day, either Oscar or Lorraine (takes, take) the car to town.
32. Neither the sound nor the rhythm (matches, match) the other stanzas in the poem.
33. Either the employees or the manager (orders, order) the inventory reduction.
34. Either the manager or the employees (orders, order) the inventory reduction.
35. (Is, Are) the children's department on this floor?
36. My daughter's passion (is, are) crafts.
37. (Was, Were) there any two-piece suits left on the rack?
38. There (isn't, aren't) many weeks left before summer.
39. Here (is, are) the data we needed.
40. Off into the sunset (runs, run) the herd of mustangs.

REVIEW

Remember the memo at the beginning of the chapter? Go back and try to correct it, then compare your version to the corrected one below. The changes are highlighted.

> To: Jessica Amerson
> From: Tyson Hall
> Re: Aides/floor nurse dispute
> Date: July 21, 2005
>
> The nurse's aides **were** having trouble with the floor nurse yesterday. He **doesn't** think he should help with unloading supplies. Every one of the aides **is** just as busy as he is. The aides think he should do his part too. They **weren't** very happy with him when he refused. Melinda and Connie **are** thinking about filing a complaint. Neither the aides nor the floor nurse **needs** this fuss. Maybe you can see if either the floor nurse or the aides **are** willing to find a better solution.

Answers

1. jokes, laugh
2. grows, grow
3. speaks, speak
4. rings, wait
5. hum, sings
6. don't
7. wasn't
8. doesn't
9. wasn't
10. doesn't, are
11. is, was
12. is
13. are
14. was
15. was
16. were
17. unlock
18. takes
19. have
20. were
21. is
22. Were
23. Does
24. Has
25. needs
26. seem
27. works
28. go
29. helps
30. causes
31. takes
32. matches
33. orders
34. order
35. Is
36. is
37. Were
38. aren't
39. is
40. runs

CHAPTER 16 GRAMMAR IQ QUIZ

Choose the correct pronoun(s) in each of the following sentences. Answers and explanations follow the quiz.

1. Chad and Roberta graded the papers from (his or her, their) classes.
2. The cat or the dog has finished (its, their) food.
3. Any woman who has cleaned out (her, their) purse knows what kind of treasures hide at the bottom.
4. Rodriquez and (he, him) went to the meeting with Janet and (I, me).
5. The supervisor is more organized than (I, me).

Answers

1. their (plural subject)
2. its (singular subject)
3. her (singular subject)
4. he, me (He went to the meeting with me.)
5. I (am)

CHAPTER

16

BEATING THE PRONOUN ODDS

Using the right pronouns in sentences can be tricky. Pronouns are misused so often in speech that few people really know how to avoid pronoun errors in writing. This chapter shows you a few tricks for getting the pronouns right every time.

Grammar concepts to know:

- **antecedent**—the noun that a pronoun replaces
- **indefinite pronouns**—pronouns that do not refer to any specific person, place, or thing
- **ambiguous reference**—words that can easily be interpreted to mean more than one thing
- **reflexive pronoun**—a pronoun that contains *self* or *selves*

Like verbs, pronouns that are misused in writing can confuse the reader. This chapter explains the basic principles of pronoun use and highlights the most common pronoun problems: agreement, incomplete constructions, reflexive pronouns, and ambiguous pronoun references.

PRONOUNS AND ANTECEDENTS

A pronoun is a word that takes the place of a noun or another pronoun. The noun represented by a pronoun is called its **antecedent**. The word *ante* means "before," and *cede* means "come." So the literal meaning of *antecedent* is "comes before." Usually, the antecedent comes before the pronoun in a sentence. In the following example sentences, the pronouns are italicized and the antecedents (the nouns they represent) are underlined.

> The state employees received *their* benefits.
> Erica thought *she* saw the stolen van and reported *it* to the authorities.
> The floor manager hates these overstocks because *he* knows *they* reduce profits.

Indefinite Pronoun Antecedents

A pronoun must agree in number with its antecedent. In other words, if the antecedent is singular, the pronoun must be singular; if the antecedent is plural, the pronoun must be plural.

People usually have little trouble matching a pronoun with a noun antecedent. However, sometimes a pronoun represents another pronoun. In the last chapter, you learned about **singular indefinite pronouns**. Remember, they are known as indefinite pronouns because they don't refer to one specific person or thing. The antecedents of singular indefinite pronouns require singular pronouns. Here is the list for your review.

each	*anyone*	*nobody*
either	*everybody*	*one*
neither	*everyone*	*somebody*
anybody	*no one*	*someone*

A pronoun with one of the words from this list as its antecedent must be singular. When the antecedent can be referring to a male or female, use the phrase *his* or *her*. In the following example sentences, the antecedent is underlined and the pronouns are italicized.

> Each [singular] of the women wore *her* [singular] favorite outfit to the ball.
> Anyone [singular] who takes up steer wrestling should pay up *his or her* [singular] life insurance.
> Someone left *her* makeup in the rest room.
> Neither of the tenants could find *his* or *her* copy of the lease.

- If two or more singular nouns or pronouns are joined by *and*, use a plural pronoun.

  Bill Gates and Sam Walton [plural] built *their* [plural] empires from scratch.
  If he and she [plural] need this information, *they* [plural] should ask me.
  When Grandma and Grandpa [plural] come to visit, *they* [plural] always bring food.

- If two or more singular nouns or pronouns are joined by *or*, use a singular pronoun.

  Trent or Jared will loan you *his* car for this errand.
  The lion or the tiger will complete *its* act.
  Remember to give Jane or Rita *her* appointment card.

- If a singular and a plural noun or pronoun are joined by *or*, the pronoun agrees with the closest noun or pronoun it represents.

  Neither the students nor the teacher [singular] brought *his* [singular] book to class.
  Neither the teacher nor the students [plural] brought *their* [plural] books to class.

Practice

Choose the correct pronoun in each of the following sentences. Check your work with the answers at the end of the chapter.

1. No one in (her, their) right mind would follow your advice.
2. Neither the soldiers nor the sergeant was sure of (his, their) location.
3. Anyone who is interested in the pilot project should sign (his or her, their) name on this contract.
4. Ask someone in maintenance to fix this desk, and (he, she, they) probably will take care of it right away.
5. Neither Gary nor Willie wants (his, their) hair cut.
6. If you shear a pin on this motor, (it, they) is hard to repair.
7. Ray knows someone who might give you (her, their) old dorm refrigerator.
8. Almost anybody can improve (his or her, their) writing by using *Grammar Essentials.*
9. If you're interested in pleasing customers, don't make (her, them) wait.
10. Arnold or Jacques will bring (his, their) recorder to tape the interview.

PRONOUNS AS SUBJECTS AND OBJECTS

A single pronoun in a sentence is easy to use correctly. In fact, most English speakers would readily identify the mistakes in the following sentences.

> **Me** worked on the project with **he**.
> Diane gave **she** a lift home.

Most people know that Me in the first sentence should be *I* and that *he* should be *him*. They would also know that *she* in the second sentence should be *her*. Such errors are easy to spot when the pronouns are used alone in a sentence. The problem occurs when a pronoun is used with a noun or another pronoun. See if you can spot the error in this sentence.

> The new machinist worked with Kirsten and I.

In the previous sentence, the word *I* should be *me*. If you turn the sentence into two separate sentences, the error becomes very obvious.

> The new machinist worked with Kirsten.
> The new machinist worked with me (not *I*).

Try to spot the errors in these three sentences.

> The teacher reprimanded my friend and I.
> Jess and me are going camping this weekend.
> The new boss assigned he and I a different campaign.

- In the first sentence, *I* should be *me*. Separate the sentences to spot the error.

> The teacher reprimanded my friend.
> The teacher reprimanded me (not *I*).

- In the second sentence, *me* should be *I*. You must change the plural verb *are* to *is* and *am* when you think of the sentences separately.

> Jess is going camping this weekend.
> I (not *me*) am going camping this weekend.

- In the third sentence, *he* and *I* should be *him* and *me*.

> The new boss assigned him (not *he*) a different campaign.
> The new boss assigned me (not *I*) a different campaign.

Splitting a sentence in two does not work as well with the preposition *between*. If you substitute *with* for *between*, then the error is easier to spot.

The disagreement is between (she, her) and (I, me).
The disagreement is with her. (not *she*)
The disagreement is with me. (not *I*)

Practice

Choose the correct pronoun in the following sentences. Check your work with the answers at the end of the chapter.

11. Bonnie and (he, him) saw the show with Bernard and (I, me).
12. Neither my children nor my husband knows what (he, they) will get me for Christmas.
13. Christine and (I, me) always clean up the lounge.
14. The conductor let (he, him) and (I, me) into the club car.
15. Did you hear the latest news about (she, her) and (they, them)?
16. Melissa and (I, me) both witnessed the accident.

NOUN-PRONOUN PAIRS

Sometimes, a noun in a sentence is immediately preceded by a pronoun. To make sure that you use the correct pronoun, delete the noun from the pair. Look at the following examples to see how this is done.

They hired (we, us) **temporary workers.**
They hired **us.**

(We, Us) **managers** threw the retirees a small party.
We threw the retirees a small party.

INCOMPLETE CONSTRUCTIONS

Sometimes, a pronoun comes at the end of a sentence following a comparative word such as *than* or *as*.

Maria spent more money than (they, them).
His young son is now taller than (I, me).
Bradley can wax floors better than (I, me).
The long walk tired us more than (they, them).

These sentences are called **incomplete constructions** because the complete meaning is only implied, not written out in its entirety. To figure out which pronoun is correct, complete the sentence in your mind and use the pronoun that makes more sense.

> Maria spent more money than *they did.*
> His young son is now taller than *I am.*

Some sentences can be completed both ways. When this is true, choose the pronoun that makes more sense.

> Bradley can play guitar better than *I can.*
> Bradley can play guitar better than *me.*

The first sentence makes more sense, so *I* is the correct pronoun.

> The long walk tired us more than *they did.*
> The long walk tired us more than *it did them.*

The second sentence makes more sense, so *them* is the correct choice.

Pronoun choice is especially important if the sentence makes sense either way. The following sentence can be completed using both pronouns, either of which makes sense. The pronoun choice controls the meaning. Choose the pronoun that conveys the intended meaning.

> I work with Assad more than (she, her).
> I work with Assad more than *she does.*
> I work with Assad more than *I work with her.*

AMBIGUOUS PRONOUN REFERENCES

Sometimes, a sentence is written in such a way that a pronoun can refer to more than one antecedent. When this happens, we say the meaning is ambiguous; that is, it can be understood in more than one way. In the following examples, the ambiguous pronouns are italicized, and the possible antecedents are underlined.

> As <u>Claude</u> spoke to the his girlfriend's <u>father</u>, *he* was very nervous.
> Take the <u>door</u> from the <u>frame</u> and paint *it.*
> <u>Theresa</u> told <u>Julia</u> *she* should get ready to go.

See how these sentences are rewritten to clarify the ambiguous references.

Claude was very nervous when he spoke to his girlfriend's father.
Paint the door after taking it off the frame.
Theresa told Julia to get ready to go.

REFLEXIVE PRONOUNS

Reflexive pronouns refer to another word that is the same individual(s) or the same thing(s). They are called **reflexive** because they reflect like a mirror. Reflexive pronouns include the word *self* or *selves: myself, yourself, himself, herself, itself, ourselves, themselves.* The following sentences show how these pronouns are used in writing.

Monica envisioned *herself* playing the lead role.
I drove *myself* to the train station.
Take care of *yourself.*
My next-door neighbors built their house *themselves.*

Using Reflexive Pronouns Correctly

- The possessive pronouns *his* and *their* cannot be made reflexive.

Wrong: The Garrets decided to supervise the building theirselves.
Correct: The Garrets decided to supervise the building themselves.

Wrong: Mitchell asked to do the work hisself.
Correct: Mitchell asked to do the work himself.

- Avoid using a reflexive pronoun when a personal pronoun works in the sentence.

Wrong: A group of volunteers and myself repaired the roof.
Correct: A group of volunteers and I repaired the roof.

Wrong: The results of the election were known only to myself.
Correct: The results of the election were known only to me.

Wrong: The responsibility is split between Jamison and yourself.
Correct: The responsibility is split between Jamison and you.

Practice

Choose the correct pronoun in each of the following sentences. Check your work with the answers that follow.

17. (We, Us) patients are pleased with our care.
18. The risk of this operation scared the doctor more than (we, us).
19. Penny and (I, me, myself) are planning a summer trip.
20. My brother drives much faster than (I, me).

Answers

1. her
2. his
3. his or her
4. he or she
5. his
6. it
7. her
8. his or her
9. them
10. his
11. he, me
12. he
13. I
14. him, me
15. her, them
16. I
17. We
18. (it scared) us
19. I
20. I (do)

CHAPTER 17 GRAMMAR IQ QUIZ

Choose the correct word from the choices in parentheses. Answers and explanations follow the quiz.

1. A deer is (laying, lying) in the tall grass.
2. The new van is (setting, sitting) in the driveway.
3. The decibel level (raises, rises) steadily throughout the concert.
4. The snake will eventually shed (its, it's) skin.
5. Tell me when (you're, your) ready to go.
6. Call the technician (that, who, which) fixed the problem last time.
7. Where is the instruction manual (that, who, which) I loaned you?
8. (Who's, Whose) coat is this?
9. Put (their, there, they're) merchandise over (their, there, they're) on the table.
10. (Their, There, They're) about to begin the session.

Answers

1. lying (resting)
2. sitting (resting)
3. rises (goes up)
4. its (belonging to it)
5. you're (you are)
6. who (use *who* for people)
7. that (use *that* for things)
8. Whose (belonging to whom)
9. their (belonging to them), there (place)
10. They're (They are)

PROBLEM VERBS AND PRONOUNS

Do *you're* and *your* confuse you? How about *lie* and *lay*, or *sit* and *set*? Knowing how to use problem words such as these correctly makes you a better writer.

Grammar concept to know:

- **possessive pronoun**—a pronoun that shows ownership (*my, your, our, their, his, hers, mine*)

This chapter covers problem verbs such as *lie/lay, sit/set, rise/raise,* and their various forms. It also covers problem pronouns such as *its/it's, your/you're, whose/who's, who/that/which,* and *there/they're/their*. You can distinguish yourself as a competent writer if you know how to use these properly.

PROBLEM VERBS

Lie/Lay

Few people use *lie* and *lay* correctly, perhaps because few people know the difference in meaning between the two. The verb *lie* means "to rest or recline." The verb *lay* means "to put or place." *Lie* is something you do yourself (or some person does himself or herself, or some object does itself); *lay* is something you do to an object.

The table that follows shows the principal parts of each of these verbs. Their meanings, written in the correct form, appear in parentheses.

Present	**Progressive** (used with *am, is, are*)	**Past**	**Past Participle** (used with *have, has,* or *had*)
lie, lies (rest, rests)	lying (resting)	lay (rested)	lain (rested)
lay, lays (place, places)	laying (placing)	laid (placed)	laid (placed)

To choose the correct form of lie or lay, simply look at the meanings in parentheses. Choose the word in parentheses that makes the most sense and use the corresponding form of lie or lay. Sometimes, none of the words seem right. In that case, choose the option that makes more sense than any of the others. If a sentence contains the word down, mentally delete the word from the sentence to make the appropriate verb more obvious. These sample sentences show how this is done.

The frisbee is _____ in the middle of the lawn. (requires progressive)
Resting makes better sense than *placing*.
Choose *lying*.

Della asked Lisa to _____ the newspaper on the kitchen table. (requires present)
Place makes better sense than *rest*.
Choose *lay*.

Yesterday, the snake _____ all day in the sun next to our house. (requires past)
Rested makes better sense than *placed*.
Choose *lay*.

Yesterday afternoon, I _____ down for a nap. (requires past)
Remove the word *down*.
Rested makes better sense than *placed*.
Choose *lay*.

Sonja remembered that she had _____ the books on her desk. (requires past participle)
Placed makes better sense than *rested*.
Choose *laid*.

Practice

Write the correct form of *lie* or *lay* in each of the blanks. Check your work with the answers at the end of the chapter.

1. Huey __________ in bed for another hour after the alarm went off.
2. __________ the papers next to the copy machine.
3. The mail __________ on the dining room table.
4. The student __________ his assignment on the teacher's desk.
5. Who knew how long the confidential documents had __________ in the open or who had __________ them there in the first place?

Sit/Set

These two verbs are very similar to *lie* and *lay. Sit* means "to rest." *Set* means "to put or place." The table below shows the principal parts of each of these verbs. Their meanings, written in the correct form, appear in parentheses.

Present	**Progressive** (used with *am, is, are*)	**Past**	**Past Participle** (used with *have, has,* or *had*)
sit, sits (rest, rests)	sitting (resting)	sat (rested)	sat (rested)
set, sets (put, place; puts, places)	setting (putting, placing)	set (put, placed)	set (placed)

Choose the correct form of *sit* or *set* by using the meanings (the words in parentheses) in the sentence first. Decide which meaning makes the most sense, then choose the corresponding form of *sit* or *set*. See how this is done in the following example sentences.

The actor __________ the props off in the wings.
Put or *placed* makes more sense than *rested.*
Choose *set.*

The judge __________ in the chair next to the bailiff.
Rested makes more sense than *put* or *placed.*
Choose *sat.*

Practice

Write the correct form of *sit* or *set* in each of the blanks. Check your work with the answers at the end of the chapter.

6. Our family __________ aside money for vacation.
7. Carol's car is the one __________ closest to the entrance.
8. Adam remembered where he __________ the packages down.
9. Scott __________ down behind to me and __________ his briefcase on the floor.
10. The parents had __________ in the waiting room for most of the morning.

Rise/Raise

The verb *rise* means "to go up." The verb *raise* means "to move something up." *Raise* requires an object. In other words, something must receive the action of the verb *raise* (raise your hand, raise the flag, raise the objection, raise children). The table that follows shows the principal parts of both verbs.

Present	**Progressive** (used with *am, is, are*)	**Past**	**Past Participle** (used with *have, has,* or *had*)
rises, rise (goes up, go up) (comes up, come	(moves up, move up)	rising (going up) (coming up)	rose (went up) (came up)
up) raises, raise		raising (moving up)	raised (moved up)

Choose the correct form of *rise* or *raise* by using the meanings (the words in parentheses) in the sentence first. Decide which meaning makes the most sense, then choose the corresponding form of *rise* or *raise.* See how this is done in the example sentences that follow. Sometimes, none of the words seem especially appropriate. In that case, choose the option that makes more sense than any of the others.

The moon __________ a little bit later each evening.
Comes up makes the most sense.
Choose *rises.*

The crowd began to __________ their voices.

Move up makes the most sense.

Choose *raise.*

The water level __________ over a foot in the last day.

Went up makes the most sense.

Choose *rose.*

Practice

Write the correct form of *rise* or *raise* in each of the blanks below. Check your answers at the end of the chapter.

11. The custodian __________ the flag every morning before the sun __________.

12. The farmer __________ corn and soybeans.

13. The fog had __________ enough for us to see beyond the next hill.

14. The church members __________ from the pews to recite a prayer.

PROBLEM PRONOUNS

Its/It's

Its is a possessive pronoun that means "belonging to it." *It's* is a contraction for *it is* or *it has.* Use *it's* only when you can also substitute the words *it is* or *it has.* Take time to make this substitution, and you will never confuse these two words.

The thermometer in the roast will measure *its* (belonging to the roast) temperature.

It's (it is) time for us to say goodbye and head home.

It's (it has) been three years now since I've seen Tom.

Practice

Choose the correct word in each set of parentheses that follow. Check your work with the answers at the end of the chapter.

15. I wonder if (its, it's) a good idea for us to be here.

16. The wind will eventually stop (its, it's) howling.

17. Tell me when (its, it's) time for a break.

18. (Its, It's) been fun to watch the dog chase (its, it's) tail.

Your/You're

Your is a possessive pronoun that means "belonging to you." *You're* is a contraction for the words *you are*. Use *you're* only when you can also substitute the words *you are*. Take time to make this substitution, and you will never confuse these two words.

> Is this *your* (belonging to you) new assignment?
> When *you're* (you are) done, I want to talk to you.
> *Your* (belonging to you) mother called this morning.
> *You're* (you are) the recipient of this year's award.

Practice

Choose the correct word in each set of parentheses that follow. Check your work with the answers at the end of the chapter.

19. (Its, It's) (your, you're) turn to do the dishes.
20. Bring (your, you're) fishing pole along if (your, you're) coming.
21. (Your, You're) scheduled to work late this evening.
22. (Your, You're) plan seems to have worked.

Who/That/Which

Who refers to people. *That* refers to things. *Which* is generally used to introduce nonessential clauses that describe things. (See Chapter 6 to review nonessential clauses.) Read the following sentences to see how each of these words is used.

- **Who** refers to people.

> There is the woman *who* designed this building.
> The man *who* fixes my car has retired.

- **That** refers to things.

> This is the neighborhood *that* I told you about.
> The print *that* I wanted has been sold.

- **Which** introduces nonessential clauses—unless they refer to people, in which case you use *who*.

> Vickie picked up a copy of *People*, *which* is her favorite magazine.
> The Mississippi River, *which* originates in Minnesota, empties into the Gulf of Mexico.
> Douglas, *who* plays in a local band, lives upstairs.
> My son, *who* loves to play video games, turns sixteen tomorrow.

Practice

Choose the correct word in each set of parentheses below. Check your work with the answers at the end of the chapter.

23. Uncle Tim is the one (who, which, that) arranged this meeting.
24. This is the coat (who, which, that) I bought last year.
25. Rod Stewart, (who, which, that) is my favorite singer, has never won a Grammy award.
26. Interstate 235, (who, which, that) runs through town, is being repaired this summer.
27. There's the young man (who, which, that) wishes to speak with you.

Whose/Who's

Whose is a possessive pronoun that means "belonging to whom." *Who's* is a contraction for the words *who is* or *who has*. Take time to make this substitution, and you will never confuse these two words.

> *Who's* (Who is) handling the funeral arrangements?
> *Whose* (belonging to whom) bright idea was that?
> This is the officer *who's* (who is) on duty tonight.
> That is the girl *whose* (belonging to whom) picture was in the paper.

There/Their/They're

There is an adverb telling where an action or item is located. *Their* is a possessive pronoun that shows ownership. *They're* is a contraction for the words *they are*. Of all the confused word groups, this one is misused most often. Here is an easy way to distinguish among these words.

- Take a close look at this version of the word *tHERE.* You can see that it contains the word *here.* Wherever you use the word *there,* you should be able to substitute the word *here,* and the sentence should still make sense.

> *There* (here) goes my future.
> The supplies are in *there* (here).

- *Their* means "belonging to them." If you can insert this phrase after *their* in a sentence and the meaning remains the same, *their* is correct.

> *Their* (belonging to them) time is limited.
> This is *their* (belonging to them) problem, not mine.

- Finally, imagine that the apostrophe in *they're* is actually a very small letter *a*. If you change *they're* to *they are* in a sentence, you'll never misuse the word. Look over the following example sentences.

    They're (they are) hoping to leave in the morning.
    Do you know how *they're* (they are) going to arrange the schedule?

Practice

Choose the correct word in each set of parentheses below. Check your work with the answers that follow.

28. (Your, You're) likely to lose your mind in (there, their, they're).
29. (There, Their, They're) rearranging the shelves in the closet.
30. (Its, It's) been a year since (there, their, they're) last anniversary.
31. The landscaper (who, which, that) did the work lives over (there, their, they're).
32. (Who's, Whose) been calling you all evening?
33. (Who's, Whose) idea was it take this shortcut?
34. Martha asked for the one (who's, whose) in charge of accounting.
35. (Who's, Whose) retirement are we celebrating?

Answers

1. lay
2. Lay
3. is lying
4. laid
5. lain, laid
6. set
7. sitting
8. set
9. sat, set
10. sat
11. raised, rose, *or* raises, rises
12. raised or raises
13. risen
14. rose
15. it's
16. its
17. it's
18. It's, its
19. It's, your
20. your, you're
21. You're
22. Your
23. who
24. that
25. who
26. which
27. who
28. You're, there
29. They're
30. It's, their
31. who, there
32. Who's
33. Whose
34. who's
35. Whose

CHAPTER 18 GRAMMAR IQ QUIZ

Choose the correct word from the parentheses in each of the following sentences. Answers follow the quiz.

1. The music sounded (strange, strangely).
2. There is a smaller (amount, number) of supporters present at this meeting.
3. Elbert tells (fewer, less) bad jokes than he used to.
4. Hugh stole the ball (clean, cleanly) from the opposing guard.
5. Anjalee danced as (good, well) as she had ever danced.
6. Caroline felt (bad, badly) after the announcement.
7. Which of these two roads is the (best, better) one to take?
8. Split the time (among, between) the twins, but share the food (among, between) all of the five children.
9. Betty is the (liveliest, most liveliest) teacher I've seen.
10. The staff (doesn't, don't) need (any, no) more stress.

Answers

1. strange
2. number
3. fewer
4. cleanly
5. well
6. bad
7. better
8. between, among
9. liveliest
10. doesn't, any

MODIFIER ETIQUETTE

Adjectives and adverbs can brighten writing and make it more specific and interesting—so that it communicates your ideas more fully. This chapter explains how to use modifiers correctly.

Grammar concepts to know:

- **modifier**—a word that describes another word
- **adjective**—a modifier that describes a noun or pronoun
- **adverb**—a modifier that describes a verb, adjective, or another adverb
- **comparative**—the form of a modifier used when comparing two things
- **superlative**—the form of a modifier used when comparing more than two things

Words that describe other words are called **modifiers. Adjectives** modify, or describe, nouns and pronouns. **Adverbs** modify, or describe, verbs, adjectives, and other adverbs. Sometimes, a group of words functions as a modifier. Modifiers play a vital part in communication. Using them correctly is an important skill.

ADJECTIVES

Adjectives describe a noun or pronoun in a sentence. Here is an easy way to tell if a word is an adjective. Adjectives answer one of three questions about another word in the sentence: *Which one? What kind?* and *How many?* The following table illustrates this. The adjectives are italicized to make them easy to identify.

Which One?	What Kind?	How Many?
the *blue* cabinet	*willow* tree	*many* hints
duct tape	*orange* vest	*five* entrances
his *first* steps	*greedy* partner	*several* reasons

Adjectives That Follow Verbs

Pay special attention to adjectives that follow verbs. Sometimes, the adjective follows a verb, but it describes a noun or pronoun that comes before the verb. The following sentences illustrate this. The italicized adjectives describe the underlined nouns.

> These <u>strawberries</u> taste *sour.* (sour strawberries)
> Rhonda's <u>change</u> of heart seemed *strange.* (strange change)
> The <u>pickles</u> are *salty.* (salty pickles)

Fewer/Less, Number/Amount

Use the adjective *fewer* to modify plural nouns, or things that can be counted. Use *less* for singular nouns that represent a quantity or a degree—things that can't be counted. Most nouns to which an *s* can be added require the adjective *fewer.*

> Our new neighborhood has *fewer* children (plural noun) than our old one had.
> Denise has *less* time (singular non-count noun) to spare than you do.

The same principle applies to the nouns *number* and *amount.* Use the noun *number* when referring to plural nouns, or things that can be counted. Use the noun *amount* when referring to nouns that are singular and can't be counted individually.

> The *number* of hours (plural noun) we estimated for this job was incorrect.
> The *amount* of time (singular noun) for our work was underestimated.

Practice

Choose the correct word in parentheses in each of the following sentences. Check your work with the answers at the end of the chapter.

1. The lawn has (fewer, less) weeds than it had last summer.
2. This side trip increased the (amount, number) of miles significantly.
3. This cutlery set costs (fewer, less) money than that one.
4. The (amount, number) of work involved does not justify the (amount, number) of people assigned to the job.
5. Phoebe remembers (fewer, less) about the old days than Grandpa does, but Grandpa tells (fewer, less) stories than Phoebe.

ADVERBS

Use adverbs to describe verbs, adjectives, and other adverbs. Here is an easy way to tell if a word is an adverb. Adverbs answer one of these questions about another word in the sentence: *Where? When? How?* and *To what extent?* The adverbs are italicized in the table that follows.

Where?	When?	How?	To What Extent?
The car drove *forward.*	Marvin left *earlier.*	She yelled *loudly.*	Royce could *hardly* wait.
Put your baggage *below.*	Hank called *later.*	Turtles move *slowly.*	Dean *narrowly* missed an accident.
Look *here.*	We'll go *tomorrow.*	The loon called *mournfully.*	Marsha *still* doesn't understand.

The next table shows examples of adverbs modifying verbs, adjectives, and other adverbs. The adverbs are italicized.

Adverbs Modifying Verbs	Adverbs Modifying Adjectives	Adverbs Modifying Other Adverbs
Packages are mailed *regularly.*	an *extremely* annoying sound	*most clearly* explained
Children play *happily.*	a *strangely* quiet room	*quite reasonably* stated
Rescuers came *immediately.*	an *unusually* clean uniform	improve *rather slowly*

ADJECTIVE OR ADVERB?

Sometimes, writers mistakenly use adjectives in place of adverbs. This is illustrated in the following sentences. The italicized words are adjectives incorrectly used in place of adverbs. The correct adverb form is in parenthesis at the end of the sentence.

Louise reads very *thorough.* (**thoroughly**)
Pack these dishes very *careful.* (**carefully**)
Vern sang as *loud* as he was able. (**loudly**)

Take special care to choose the correct word when using verbs that deal with the senses: *touch, taste, look, smell, sound.* If the word following the verb describes a noun or pronoun that comes before the verb, use an adjective. If the word following the verb describes the verb, use an adverb.

In each of the sets of examples that follow, the same verb is used. In one sentence, however, the word following the verb is an adjective. In the other sentence, the word following is an adverb. The parentheses explain how the word is used. Read the examples and take note of the differences.

The trainer felt gently around the player's ankle. (*Gently* is an adverb describing *felt.*)
The entire group felt sick after lunch. (*Sick* is an adjective describing *group.*)

The judge looked skeptical after the witness testified. (*Skeptical* is an adjective describing *judge.*)
The judge looked skeptically at the attorney. (*Skeptically* is an adverb describing *looked.*)

The milk smelled sour to us. (*Sour* is an adjective describing *milk.*)
The doe smelled the feed hesitantly. (*Hesitantly* is used as an adverb describing *smelled.*)

Practice

Choose the correct word in parentheses in each of the following sentences. Check your work with the answers at the end of the chapter.

6. Anita sang the melody line (correct, correctly).
7. Patricia looked (tired, tiredly) after the long day.
8. This door doesn't shut as (easy, easily) as it used to.
9. These new boots feel more (comfortable, comfortably) than my old ones.

10. Ask (polite, politely) if you need help with your work.
11. The doctor walked (slow, slowly) out of the operating room.
12. Jay seems (unhappy, unhappily) about the test results.
13. The woman looked (angry, angrily) as she left the hair salon.
14. The burglar felt (careful, carefully) for the alarm switch.
15. The steam treatment cleaned our carpets (thorough, thoroughly).

Good and Well, Bad and Badly

Good and *bad* are adjectives. *Well* and *badly* are adverbs. Sometimes, *good* and *bad* are mistakenly used to describe a verb. Use *well* and *badly* to describe an action.

> Elizabeth performed *well* (or *badly)* at her recital. (*Well* or *badly* describes *performed,* a verb.)
> Carolyn felt *good* (or *bad*) after her treatment. (*Good* or *bad* describes *Carolyn,* a noun.)
> The condominiums were *well* (or *badly*) built. (*Well* or *badly* describes *built,* a verb.)
> The coffee smelled *good* (or *bad)* when I walked into the house. (*Good* or *bad* describes *coffee,* a noun.)

Practice

Choose the correct word in parentheses in each of the following sentences. Check your work with the answers at the end of the chapter.

16. Pasta does not taste as (good, well) if it is overcooked.
17. Paulina felt (bad, badly) after the workout.
18. Janelle did (good, well) on her annual performance review.
19. This new arrangement works very (good, well).
20. The touring choir sang quite (bad, badly).

COMPARISONS

Adjectives and adverbs change form when they are used in comparisons. When you compare two things, use the comparative form of the modifier. If you are comparing more than two things, use the superlative form of the modifier.

Creating the Comparative Form

To compare two things, you can either:

- add *er* to the modifier, or
- place the word *more* or *less* before the modifier

Add *-er* to most short modifiers (one or two syllables). Use *more* and *less* with modifiers that have more than two syllables.

Creating the Superlative Form

To compare more than two things, you can either:

- add *-est* to the modifier, or
- place the word *most* or *least* before the modifier

Add *-est* to most short modifiers (one or two syllables). Use *more* or *most* with modifiers that are more than two syllables.

Between/Among

When comparing items in a prepositional phrase, use *between* for two items, *among* for three or more.

Look at the samples in the following table. Some modifiers change form completely. The first six lines of the table illustrate these special modifiers.

Modifier	**Comparative** (for two items)	**Superlative** (more than two items)
good	better	best
well	better	best
many	more	most
much	more	most
bad	worse	worst
little	less or lesser	least
neat	neater	neatest
lovely	lovelier	loveliest
funny	funnier	funniest
extreme	more [or less]extreme	most [or least] extreme
intelligent	more [or less] intelligent	most [or least] intelligent
precisely	more [or less] precisely	most [or least] precisely
	between	among

See how the comparative and superlative forms are used in the following sentences.

I like pumpkin pie *better* than key lime pie. (compares two pies)

If you think Jane is a bad tennis player, just wait until you see her sister Jess play—she is even *worse*. (compares two tennis players—Jane and Jess)

Many people love Venice, but I found Rome to be a *more beautiful city*. (compares two cities with a modifier that has more than two syllables)

Matthew is the *neatest* of the three siblings. (compares more than two siblings)

Practice

Choose the correct word in parentheses in each of the following sentences. Check your work with the answers at the end of the chapter.

21. The Ford Taurus is the (large, larger, largest) selling mid-size car.
22. Heavy cover is the (more, most) promising habitat for pheasants.
23. Charlotte is the (younger, youngest) of the twins and the (shorter, shortest) one in the entire family.
24. Divide my land (among, between) my two sons, but split the money (among, between) all of my children.
25. The decorator chose the (more, most) unusual color scheme I've ever seen.

Avoiding Illogical or Unclear Comparisons

"Cassidy is braver than any Western hero," is an illogical statement. It implies that Cassidy, who is a Western hero, is braver than himself. Always include the words *other* or *else* to keep your comparisons from being illogical.

Cassidy is braver than any **other** Western hero.
Sid can track better than anyone **else** in the group.

Avoiding Double Comparisons

A double comparison occurs when a writer uses both *-er* or *-est* and *more/less* or *most/least*.

Wrong	Correct
Horace is the most rudest man I know.	Horace is the rudest man I know.
These instructions are more clearer.	These instructions are clearer.
Ethel is more pickier about her kitchen than I am.	Ethel is pickier about her kitchen than I am.

AVOIDING DOUBLE NEGATIVES

When a negative word such as *not* or *no* is added to a statement that is already negative, a double negative results. Avoid double negatives in your writing. The words *hardly* and *barely* are also negative words. In the following example sentences, the negative words are highlighted. Pay close attention to how the incorrect sentences are rewritten to avoid the double negative.

Wrong	Correct
The store **doesn't** have **no** nails that size.	The store **doesn't** have any nails that size. The store has **no** nails that size.
We **don't** want **no** dessert.	We **don't** want any dessert. We want **no** dessert.
I **don't barely** have money for a soda.	I **don't** have money for a soda. I **barely** have money for a soda.
I **can't hardly** hear you.	I can **hardly** hear you. I **can't** hear you.

MISPLACED MODIFIERS

Place words, phrases, or clauses that describe nouns and pronouns as closely as possible to the words they describe. Failure to do this often results in a **misplaced modifier** and a sentence that means something other than what was intended.

Placement of Words That Modify

The words *only, almost,* and *just* should be placed as close as possible to the word described. The best place is right before the words they describe. The placement of the word, phrase, or clause affects the meaning of the sentence.

The woman **only** looked at two chairs.
The woman looked at **only** two chairs.

The first sentence implies that the woman "only looked" at the chairs, but nothing else; she didn't sit in them or touch them. The second sentence explains that she looked at "only two" samples, not three or four. The placement of the word *only* changes the meaning of the sentence.

Look at another pair of sentences:

Josh **nearly** scored four touchdowns.
Josh scored **nearly** four touchdowns.

In the first sentence, Josh "nearly scored," or came very close to the goal line four times without actually crossing. In the second sentence, Josh scored "nearly four" touchdowns—maybe three and a half. How many points are awarded for that?

Here's an example using *just:*

The delivery company **just** rents its vans.
The delivery company rents **just** its vans.

In the first sentence of the previous example, the company "just rents" its vans, rather than buying them. The second sentence suggests that the company rents "just its vans," not any of its other vehicles, perhaps cars or trucks.

Placement of Phrases and Clauses That Modify

Phrases and clauses that describe nouns or pronouns must also be placed as closely as possible to the words they describe. The sentences in the next table contain misplaced modifiers. Pay close attention to how they are rewritten to clarify the meaning.

Sentences with Misplaced Modifiers	Corrected Versions
My uncle told me about feeding cattle in the kitchen. (What are cattle doing in the kitchen?)	In the kitchen, my uncle told me about feeding cattle. My uncle told me about feeding cattle while we were in the kitchen.
A huge python followed the man that was slithering slowly through the grass. (Why was the man slithering through the grass?)	A huge python that was slithering slowly through the grass followed the man. Slithering slowly through the grass, a huge python followed the man.

DANGLING MODIFIERS

Words, phrases, or clauses that begin a sentence and are set off by commas sometimes don't clearly modify any word or group of words in a sentence. These are called **dangling modifiers.** The sentences in the following table contain dangling modifiers. Pay close attention to how they are rewritten to avoid the problem.

Sentences with Dangling Modifiers	Corrected Versions
While talking on the telephone, the potatoes boiled over. (Why were the potatoes talking on the telephone?)	While I was talking on the telephone, the potatoes boiled over. The potatoes boiled over while I talked on the phone.
Nailed to a utility pole, Jason saw the sign. (Why was Jason nailed to a utility pole?)	Jason saw the sign nailed to a utility pole. Nailed to the utility pole, the sign was visible to Jason.
Broken and beyond repair, Grandma threw the serving dish away. (Why was Grandma broken?)	Grandma threw away the broken serving dish that was beyond repair. Broken and beyond repair, the serving dish was thrown away by Grandma.

Practice

Choose the correctly written sentence from each of the following sets. Check your answers on the next page.

26. **a.** Sylvan likes eggs fried in butter.
b. Fried in butter, Sylvan likes eggs.

27. **a.** Janette likes fresh fish better than any meat.
b. Janette likes fresh fish better than any other meat.

28. **a.** At the age of three, Grandpa took me fishing.
b. When I was three, Grandpa took me fishing.

29. **a.** Dennis is quicker than anybody on the team. (Dennis is a team member.)
b. Dennis is quicker than anybody else on the team.

30. **a.** I can't hardly understand why we're still waiting.
b. I can't understand why we're still waiting.

31. **a.** Growling softly, a big dog approached the boy.
b. A big dog approached the boy that was growling softly.

32. **a.** This floor doesn't need no more wax.
b. This floor doesn't need any more wax.

33. **a.** The speaker would only answer two questions.
b. The speaker would answer only two questions.

34. **a.** While barbecuing our steaks, a hungry salesman walked into the backyard.
b. A hungry salesman walked into the backyard while we were barbecuing our steaks.

35. **a.** Swinging from branch to branch, I saw the spider monkey.
b. I saw the spider monkey swinging from branch to branch.

Answers

1. fewer
2. number
3. less
4. amount, number
5. less, fewer
6. correctly
7. tired
8. easily
9. comfortable
10. politely
11. slowly
12. unhappy
13. angry
14. carefully
15. thoroughly
16. good
17. bad
18. well
19. well
20. badly
21. largest
22. most
23. younger, shortest
24. between, among
25. most
26. a.
27. b.
28. b.
29. b.
30. b.
31. a.
32. b.
33. b.
34. b.
35. b.

CHAPTER 19 GRAMMAR IQ QUIZ

Choose the correct word in parentheses in each of the following sentences. Answers follow the quiz.

1. Make sure to use your right foot to step on the (break, brake).
2. It's right in front of your eyes, in (plane, plain) sight.
3. It took me a (weak, week) to strip the desk of all five layers of paint.
4. Craig (knew, new) about the surprise party.
5. Can you (here, hear) what the speaker is saying?
6. How do you think the news will (affect, effect) her?
7. He (choose, chose) another line of questioning.
8. If you don't start moving better, we will surely (loss, lose, loose) this match.
9. Brian is arriving at work later (then, than) he (use, used) to.
10. This package is (supposed, suppose) to contain the receipt.

Answers

1. brake
2. plain
3. week
4. knew
5. hear
6. affect
7. chose
8. lose
9. than, used
10. supposed

TRICKY WORDS

Brake or *break? Than* or *then? Accept* or *except?* This chapter explains the meanings of easily confused words. If you keep track of the meanings, you can avoid misusing these words in your writing. This chapter makes it easy to do just that.

Grammar concepts to know:

- **verb**—a word that shows action or otherwise helps to complete the meaning of a sentence
- **noun**—the name of a person, place, thing, or idea
- **preposition**—a word that shows a relationship between a noun or pronoun and another word in the sentence

This chapter explains some of the most commonly confused word pairs. If you learn to distinguish between these words, you can avoid errors in your writing. The words are divided into five separate sections, with practice exercises at the end of each section.

PART ONE

Brake/Break

- *Brake* as a verb means to *slow* or *stop*. As a noun it means "a device that slows or stops action."
- *Break* as a verb means to *separate, shatter, adjourn*. As a noun, it means *a(n) separation, crack, pause,* or *opportunity.*

During our *break* (pause) we asked the sergeant if we could *break* (separate) rank.

Brake (slow) gently if you're on packed snow by applying slight pressure to the *brake* (device).

Dustin Hoffman's big *break* (opportunity) came when he took a role in *Midnight Cowboy.*

Passed/Past

- *Passed* is a verb, the past tense of *pass,* meaning *transferred, went ahead,* or *by, elapsed,* or *finished.*
- *Past* as a noun means *history*. As an adjective it means *former*.

It's best not to dig up the *past* (history) in this family.

An hour *passed* (elapsed) before the X-rays returned from the lab.

Mae *passed* (finished) the test she took yesterday.

Ken Griffey *passed* (transferred) his baseball talent to his son.

I know I lived near water in a *past* (former) life.

The race cars *passed* (went by) the stands at over 200 miles per hour.

Peace/Piece

- *Peace* is a noun meaning *tranquility*.
- *Piece* as a noun means *division, bit,* or *creation*. As a verb, it means *to patch,* or *repair.*

We could have some *peace* (tranquility) around here if you would just *piece* (patch) together the few remaining *pieces* (bits) of your mind.

Plain/Plane

- *Plain* as an adjective means *ordinary, clear,* or *simple.* As a noun, it means *flat country.*
- *Plane* is a noun meaning *airship, flat surface,* or *level.*

Nomadic tribes roamed the *plain* (flat country).
Helen prefers *plain* (ordinary) vegetables.
The answer is *plain* (clear) to me.
The commune adopted a very *plain* (simple) lifestyle.
The pilot flew the *plane* (airship) on a *plane* (level).

Scene/Seen

- *Scene* is a noun meaning *view, site,* or *commotion.*
- *Seen* is a verb, the past participle of *see,* meaning *observed* or *noticed.*

The crowd caused a *scene* (commotion) at the *scene* (site) of the fight, the most confused sight the rookie officer had ever *seen* (observed).

Practice

Choose the correct word in each of the following sentences. Check your work with the answers at the end of the chapter.

1. Cedric hit the (brake, break) as he noticed the truck ahead (brake, break) to avoid a (brake, break) in the road.
2. The rookie second baseman (passed, past) the record set in the (passed, past) year.
3. We hope this (peace, piece) of information will give you (peace, piece) of mind.
4. The (plain, plane) gasoline won't work to fuel this (plain, plane).
5. Scottie's parents hadn't (scene, seen) the most violent (scene, seen) in the show.

PART TWO

By/Buy

- *By* is a preposition used to introduce a phrase: *by the book, by the time,* or *by the way.*
- *Buy* as a verb means *to purchase*. As a noun, it means *a bargain* or *deal.*

Carter stopped *by* (preposition) the store to *buy* (purchase) some albums he thought were a great *buy* (deal).

Dear/Deer

- *Dear* is an adjective meaning *valued* or *loved.*
- *Deer* is a noun referring to a four-legged animal that lives in the woods and looks like Bambi.

The *dear* (loved) car was totaled when it struck a *deer* (animal).

Die/Dye

- *Die* is a verb meaning *pass away* or *fade.*
- *Dye* as a verb means *to color* or *tint.* As a noun, it means *coloring* or *pigment.*

The speaker waited for the noise to *die* (fade).
We plan to *dye* (color) the shirts orange.

Weak/Week

- *Weak* is an adjective meaning *flimsy, frail,* or *powerless.*
- *Week* is a noun meaning *seven days.*

The signal from the lost plane was so *weak* (frail) that rescuers took a *week* (seven days) to locate the survivors.

Which/Witch

- *Which* is a pronoun. Use *which* in a sentence dealing with a choice: *Which* one do you want? Also, use *which* to introduce a nonessential clause.

This car, *which* I have never driven, is the one I'm thinking about buying.

- *Witch* is a noun meaning *sorceress* or *enchantress.*

Can you tell me *which* (choice word) *witch* (enchantress) to believe?

Practice

Choose the correct word in each of the following sentences. Check your work with the answers at the end of the chapter.

6. If the fax machine isn't repaired (by, buy) morning, we'll have to (by, buy) another one.
7. We waited to (die, dye) the sheets, hoping the wind would (die, dye) down.
8. This animal is too (weak, week) to survive for more than a (weak, week).
9. My (dear, deer) child, you'll never see a (dear, deer) if you watch the sky.
10. The (which, witch) couldn't decide (which, witch) cat to take on Halloween.

PART THREE

Hear/Here

- *Hear* is a verb meaning *listen to.*
- *Here* means *in this place* or *to this place.*

Come *here* (to this place) so you can *hear* (listen to) this recording.

Hole/Whole

- *Hole* is a noun meaning *opening, gap,* or *dent.*
- *Whole* as an adjective means *entire* or *intact.* As a noun, it means *entire part* or *amount.*

The *whole* (entire) pie was eaten.
The attendant repaired the *hole* (opening) in the tire.

Knew/New

- *Knew* (the past tense of *know,)* is a verb, meaning *understood* or *recognized.*
- *New* is an adjective meaning *fresh, different,* or *current.*

I *knew* (understood) he was looking for a *new* (different) approach.

Know/No

- *Know* is a verb meaning *to understand* or *recognize.*
- *No* means *not so, not any,* or *not at all.* As an adjective, it means *none* or *not one.*

I *know* (understand) that we have *no* (not any) more money in this account.

Meat/Meet

- *Meat* is a noun meaning *food, flesh,* or *main part.*
- *Meet* as a verb means *assemble, greet,* or *fulfill.* As a noun, it means *assembly.*

The chefs will *meet* (assemble) to select the *meat* (flesh) for the dinner.

Practice

Choose the correct word in each of the following sentences. Check your work with the answers at the end of the chapter.

11. You'll (hear, here) better if you stand (hear, here).
12. This (hole, whole) means this (hole, whole) balloon is worthless.
13. Hans was the only one who (knew, new) how to operate the (knew, new) press.
14. I (know, no) we expect (know, no) further trouble from you.
15. The hunters will (meat, meet) at the locker plant to split up the (meat, meet) from the deer.

PART FOUR

Advice/Advise

- *Advice,* a noun meaning *suggestion* or *suggestions.*
- *Advise* is a verb meaning *suggest to* or *warn.*

We *advise* (warn) you to heed the *advice* (suggestions) of your attorney.

Affect/Effect

- *Affect* as a verb means *alter, inspire, move emotionally,* or *imitate.* As an adjective, it means *imitated* or *pretended.*
- *Effect* as a noun means *consequence* or *result.* As a verb, it means *cause.*

King's moving "I Have a Dream" speech will *affect* (inspire) listeners for many generations.
How will this *affect* (alter) the outcome?
Merle's *affected* (pretended) accent annoyed his friends.
What *effect* (consequence) does cold weather have on tropical plants?
Will it *effect* (cause) a change?

One/Won

- *One* is an adjective meaning *single.* It can also be used as pronoun to replace a person, place, or thing.
- *Won* is verb meaning *prevailed, achieved,* or *acquired.*

Lynette is the *one* (referring to Lynette) who *won* (acquired) over *one* (single) million dollars in the lottery.

Seam/Seem

- *Seam* is a noun meaning *joint* or *joining point.*
- *Seem* is a verb meaning *appear.*

It *seems* (appears) to me that this *seam* (joining point) is coming apart.

Weather/Whether

- *Weather* is a noun referring to the condition outside.
- *Whether* means *if* and is used when referring to a possibility or choice.

We won't know *whether* (if) we'll come until we know what the *weather* (condition outside) is going to do.

Practice

Choose the correct word in each of the following sentences. Check your work with the answers at the end of the chapter.

16. The psychic will (advice, advise) you to seek (advice, advise) often.
17. We won't know the (affect, effect) of this change on production until we know how it will (affect, effect) worker morale.
18. If I (one, won) the match, I would be the only (one, won) to have (one, won) more than (one, won) championship ring.
19. Does this (seam, seem) (seam, seem) loose to you?
20. Do you know (weather, whether) this awful (weather, whether) will continue into tomorrow?

PART FIVE

Choose/Chose

- *Choose* is a verb meaning *to select.* It rhymes with *bruise.*
- *Chose* is also a verb, the past tense of *choose,* meaning *selected.*

The neighbors *chose* (selected) not to participate in the neighborhood party.
Next time, they should *choose* (select) more wisely.

Loose/Lose/Loss

- *Loose* is an adjective meaning *free, unrestrained,* or *not tight.* It rhymes with *goose.*
- *Lose* is a verb meaning to *misplace,* to *be defeated,* or *fail to keep.* It rhymes with *shoes.*
- *Loss* is a noun meaning the *opposite of victory or gain, defeat,* or *downturn.* It rhymes with *toss.*

The cattle ran *loose* (free) in the pasture.
The knot in this shoelaces is *loose* (not tight).
If you *lose* (misplace) your place in line, it means a serious *loss* (opposite of gain) of time.

Than/Then

- *Than* is a conjunctive word used to make a comparison.
- *Then* means *next* or tells when.

First, we'll eat; *then* (next) we'll discuss ways to make this season more successful *than* (comparison) our last one.

Suppose/Supposed

- *Suppose* is a verb meaning *assume* or *imagine.*
- *Supposed* (the past tense of *suppose,*) is a verb, meaning *assumed* or *imagined.* As an adjective, it means *expected* or *obligated.*

I *suppose* (assume) we can finish this load.
The bricklayers *supposed* (assumed) the foundation would be ready.
The concrete was *supposed* (expected) to have cured by morning.

Use/Used

- *Use* as a verb means *utilize* or *deplete.* As a noun, it means *purpose.*
- *Used* (the past tense of *use,*) is a verb meaning *utilized* or *depleted.* As an adjective, it means *secondhand.*
- *Used to* means *accustomed to* or *formerly.*

> You can *use* (utilize) the same process you *used* (utilized) yesterday.
>
> What is the *use* (purpose) of buying *used* (secondhand) equipment if it doesn't work?
>
> We *used to* (formerly) talk regularly before we became *used to* (accustomed to) long periods of silence.

Practice

Choose the correct word in each of the following sentences. Check your work with the answers on the next page.

21. (Choose, Chose) your words carefully.
22. Nigel (choose, chose) not to participate in the games.
23. A (loose, lose, loss) today means we'll (loose, lose, loss) our first place spot.
24. The turkeys ran (loose, lose, loss) in the yard.
25. The joint should remain (loose, lose, loss) so you won't (loose, lose, loss) flexibility.
26. Don't (loose, lose, loss) your gloves.
27. Luann was (suppose, supposed) to come earlier today (than, then) yesterday.
28. We (use, used) to look at (use, used) cars, but now we've become (use, used) to driving new vehicles.
29. (Choose, Chose) your racket; (then, than) go change your clothes.
30. Spending a quiet evening at home is more appealing (than, then) it (use, used) to be.

Answers

1. brake, brake, break
2. passed, past
3. piece, peace
4. plain, plane
5. seen, scene
6. by, buy
7. dye, die
8. weak, week
9. dear, deer
10. witch, which
11. hear, here
12. hole, whole
13. knew, new
14. know, no
15. meet, meat
16. advise, advice
17. effect, affect
18. won, one, won, one
19. seam, seem
20. whether, weather
21. Choose
22. chose
23. loss, lose
24. loose
25. loose, lose
26. lose
27. supposed, than
28. used, used, used
29. Choose, then
30. than, used

CHAPTER 20 GRAMMAR IQ QUIZ

Choose the correct word in parentheses in each of the following sentences. Answers follow the quiz.

1. Jonelle was (to, too, two) short (to, too, two) ride (to, too, two) of the rides at the park.
2. (Their, They're, There) going to sit over (their, they're, there), by (their, they're, there) luggage.
3. (Wear, Where, Were) did you buy your sofa?
4. It was (quit, quiet, quite) an accomplishment to get the group of four-year-olds to (quit, quiet, quite) playing and be totally (quit, quiet, quite) for story time.
5. My parents (expect, accept, except) me to (expect, accept, except) the terms of my project (expect, accept, except) for the due date, which is too soon.
6. Ben acts as (though, threw, through) Jen (though, threw, through) the ball (though, threw, through) the window on purpose.
7. Claire was (all ready, already) with an answer to my rebuttal.
8. You spent (all together, altogether) too much money trying to get the family (all together, altogether) for Thanksgiving.
9. (Every day, Everyday) when I get home, I change into my (every day, everyday) clothes to walk my Chihuahua.
10. If we book our tickets now, (maybe, may be) we can get a better rate.

Answers

1. too, to, to, two
2. They're, their, there
3. Where
4. quite, quit, quiet
5. expect, accept, except
6. though, threw, through
7. all ready
8. altogether, all together
9. Every day, everyday
10. maybe

CHAPTER 20 MORE TRICKY WORDS

This chapter covers more confusing words: those that have three easily confused meanings and those that are sometimes written as one word and sometimes as two. By the end of this chapter, you'll know which ones to use and why.

Here are some more of the most commonly confused words that you are likely to use in your writing. If you learn to distinguish these words, you can avoid errors. The words are divided into three separate sections, with practice exercises at the end of each section.

THREE-WAY CONFUSION

To/Too/Two

- *To* is a preposition or part of an infinitive (used with a verb).

  Preposition: Use *to* for introducing a prepositional phrase that tells *where:* to the store, to the top, to my home, to our garden, to his laboratory, to his castle, to our advantage, to an open door, to a song, to the science room, etc.

Part of an infinitive: Use *to* as part of an infinitive (*to* followed by a verb, sometimes separated by an adverb): to run, to jump, to want badly, to seek, to propose, to write, to explode, to sorely need, to badly botch, to carefully examine, and so on.

- *Too* is an adverb meaning *also* or *very*. Wherever you use the word *too,* you should be able to substitute the word *also* or *very.*
- *Two* is an adjective, the name of a number, as in *one, two.*

The couple went *to* (introduces a prepositional phrase) the deli *to* (introduces an infinitive phrase) pick up *two* (one, two) plate dinners because both of them were *too* (very) tired *to* (introduces an infinitive phrase) cook dinner.

There/Their/They're

- *There* is an adverb that refers to a the location of something or someone. Whenever you use the word *there,* you should also be able to substitute the word *here.*
- *Their* means "belonging to them." Use it as an adjective to show possession.
- *They're* is a short form, or contraction, of the words *they are.* Use *they're* only when you could also use the words *they are.*

They're (they are) going *there* (a location) to see *their* (belonging to them) doctor.

If *their* (belonging to them) children are in *there* (a location), *they're* (they are) in trouble.

Lead/Led/Lead

- *Lead* as a verb means to *guide* or *direct.* As a noun, it means *front position.* It rhymes with *seed.*
- *Led* is a verb, the past tense of *lead*, meaning *guided* or *directed.* It rhymes with *red.*
- *Lead* is also a noun, the name of a metal. It, too, rhymes with *red.*

The Pied Piper took the *lead* (front position) and *led* (guided) the children out of Hamlin.

The presence of *lead* (a metal) in the paint *led* (directed) us to think the house was old.

Quite/Quit/Quiet

- *Quite* is an adverb meaning *completely, very,* or *entirely*. It rhymes with *bite*.
- *Quit* is a verb meaning *stop, cease* or *stopped, ceased*. It rhymes with *sit*.
- *Quiet* as an adjective means *calm, silent, noiseless*. As a verb, it means to *soothe* or *calm*. As a noun, it means *tranquillity* or *peacefulness*. It rhymes with *riot*.

Mother was *quite* (very) shocked when the children *quit* (stopped) playing and spent some *quiet* (calm) time in their rooms.

Where/Wear/Were

- *Where* is an adverb referring to a place or location.
- *Wear* as a verb means to *put on, tire,* or *deteriorate*. As a noun, it means *deterioration*.
- *Were* is a verb, the plural past tense of *be*.

Where (a place) are the parts that showed excessive *wear* (deteriortion)?

You will *wear* (deteriorate) out this coat if you *wear* (put on) it all the time.

Where (location) are the clothes you *were* (helping verb) planning to *wear (put on)* tomorrow?

Practice

Choose the correct form of the word in parentheses. Check your work with the answers at the end of the chapter.

1. Along with the lettuce, please get (to, too, two) avocados (to, too, two) when you go (to, too, two) the store.
2. They should put (there, their, they're) luggage in (there, their, they're).
3. If (there, their, they're) interested in improving (there, their, they're) health, I'll help them get (there, their, they're).
4. Two hours is (quiet, quit, quite) a long time for children to be (quiet, quit, quite).
5. The furnace (quiet, quit, quite) during the night, and it's (quiet, quit, quite) cold in the house.
6. Do you know (wear, were, where) I could (wear, were, where) something like this?
7. The horses (wear, were, where) restless today.

8. Ronald couldn't remember (wear, were, where) the cards (wear, were, where).
9. The foreman (led, lead) the workers out of the (led, lead) mine.
10. Kevin mounted the (led, lead) horse and (led, lead) the wagons into the mountains.

MORE THREE-WAY CONFUSION

Accept/Except/Expect

- *Accept* is a verb meaning *to receive* or *bear.*
- *Except* is a preposition meaning *but,* or *excluding.*
- *Expect* is a verb meaning *anticipate, demand,* or *assume.*

Customers *expect* (demand) nothing *except* (but) a fair deal, I *expect* (assume).

We *expect* (anticipate) they will *accept* (receive) our apology.

Lorraine will *accept* (bear) the responsibility for making housing arrangements.

Right/Write/Rite

- *Right* is an adjective meaning *correct, proper,* or the *opposite of left.*
- *Write* is a verb meaning *record* or *inscribe.*
- *Rite* is a noun meaning *ceremony* or *ritual.*

The court reporter will *write* (record) the exact words of the testimony.

The shaman will be able to perform the *rite* (ceremony) in the *right* (proper) way.

It seems *right* (proper) that we record the *right* (correct) answer on the *right* (opposite of left) side.

Though/Through/Threw

- *Though* as a conjunction means *even if.* As an adverb, it means *however.*
- *Through* means *from one side to the other.*
- *Threw* is the past tense of the verb *throw.* It means *tossed.*

Though (even if) you may think it's a waste, you should *throw* (toss) away outdated medication.

Bibek *threw* (tossed) the ball *through* (from one side to the other) the window.

Sent/Cent/Scent

- *Sent* (the past tense of *send,*) is a verb meaning *dispatched* or *transmitted.*
- *Cent* is a noun meaning *one penny*, a coin worth one-hundredth of a dollar.
- *Scent* is a noun meaning *odor* or *smell.*

You can buy this *scent* (odor) capsule for just a *cent* (one penny).
The guide *sent* (dispatched) a message as soon as the dogs picked up the *scent* (odor).

Sight/Site/Cite

- *Sight* as a noun means the *ability to see.* As a verb, it means *see* or *spot.*
- *Site* is a noun meaning *location* or *position.*
- *Cite* is a verb meaning *quote* or *make reference to.*

At ninety, the old man's *sight* (ability to see) was sharp enough to *sight* (spot) even the smallest flaw.
This is the proposed *site* (location) for our school.
Cite (make reference to) the source of the information in your paper.

Practice

Choose the correct form of the word in parentheses. Check your work with the answers at the end of the chapter.

11. Our letter can be (sent, cent, scent) if we add another (sent, cent, scent) of postage.
12. Bernice smelled the (sent, cent, scent) of cabbage when she walked into the kitchen.
13. The customers were (right, write, rite) in assuming the company would (right, write, rite) them a letter explaining the policy change.
14. The senior prom is a (right, write, rite) of passage.
15. The manufacturers (accept, except, expect) that we will (accept, except, expect) a partial delivery or our order.
16. The doctor walked (though, through, threw) the waiting room even (though, through, threw) the receptionist (though, through, threw) a fit every time she did so.
17. The quarterback (though, through, threw) the ball right (though, through, threw) the hands of the receiver.
18. Beyond the next hill you should be able to (sight, site, cite) the (sight, site, cite) for the new city park.

19. Researchers hope that their statistics will be (sighted, sited, cited) accurately.

20. Everyone (accept, except, expect) John Henry will (accept, except, expect) our proposal.

ONE WORD OR TWO?

The words in this next section are very much alike but have different meanings, depending on whether they are one word or two words.

Already/All Ready

- *Already* means *as early as this, previously,* or *by this time.*
- *All ready* means *completely ready* or *totally ready.*

The dockhands had unloaded the warehouse *already* (as early as this).
The harvesters have *already* (previously, by this time) finished that field.
Is this print order *all ready* (completely ready) to go?

Altogether/All Together

- *Altogether* means *entirely* or *completely.*
- *All together* means *simultaneously.*

His testimony was *altogether* (entirely) true.
The fans moaned *all together* (simultaneously).

Everyday/Every Day

- *Everyday* means *ordinary* or *usual.*
- *Every day* means *each day.*

I wore my *everyday* (ordinary) clothes.
Inspectors examine the machinery *every day* (each day).

Maybe/May Be

- *Maybe* means *perhaps.*
- *May be* means *might be.*

Maybe (perhaps) we will finish a day earlier than we had planned.
On the other hand, we *may be* (might be) later than we thought.

ALWAYS TWO WORDS

The words in this section are often incorrectly written as one word.

All Right

Alright is substandard usage. Avoid using this form in formal writing.

- *All right* means *completely fine* or *entirely good.*

Your work seems *all right* (completely fine) to me.

A Lot/Allot

Alot is substandard usage. Avoid using this form in formal writing.

- *A lot* means *much.*
- *Allot* is a verb meaning to *portion out.*

The committee should *allot* (portion out) *a lot* of (much) time for questions.

Practice

Choose the correct form of the word in parentheses. Check your work with the answers on the next page.

21. You (where, wear, were) your (everyday, every day) shoes almost (everyday, every day).

22. (Maybe, may be) if we change our approach, it (maybe, may be) the thing that will help us get back on track.

23. If the whole section had been (already, all ready) we could have (already, all ready) started.

24. They should be (alright, all right) if they read the directions.

25. If we get the whole family (altogether, all together), we should have (altogether, all together) enough people power to finish moving.

26. Chester thought it was (all right, alright) to (a lot, allot) a few tickets for family members.

27. Patrick has (a lot, allot) of spare change.

28. Keith has (all ready, already) picked up our mail, but (may be, maybe) we can catch him before he leaves.

29. Guy (may be, maybe) able to deliver this speech if he can get his notes (all together, altogether).

30. Margaret leaves at 3:30 (every day, everyday).

Answers

1. two, too, to
2. their, there
3. they're, their, there
4. quite, quiet
5. quit, quite
6. where, wear
7. were
8. where, were
9. led, lead
10. lead, led
11. sent, cent
12. scent
13. right, write
14. rite
15. expect, accept
16. through, though, threw
17. threw, through
18. sight, site
19. cited
20. except, accept
21. wear, everyday, every day
22. Maybe, may be
23. all ready, already
24. all right
25. all together, altogether
26. all right, allot
27. a lot
28. already, maybe
29. may be, all together
30. every day

CONCLUSION

You've done it! You've made it through these lessons. Now you can take the Grammar IQ Final Exam that follows, with confidence! Check your answers at the end of the exam. In addition, if you have trouble with verbs in English, you should refer to Appendix A, "Two-Word Verbs," which tells you how to use certain idiomatic verb forms. If you had fun or want to learn even more about writing, look at Appendix B, "Additional Resources."

Now it's time to reap a return on the money you invested in this book. Here's how: Write a memo asking for a raise. If you can do that, you know the time you've spent with this book has been worth your while. Go ahead, do it. The worst thing that can happen is that your request will be denied. Even if this happens, your writing will have made an impression. If you presented a few good arguments, your supervisor will remember them. Your next raise will probably come sooner as a result. The best thing that can happen, of course, is that you will get a raise. How can you lose? Even if you don't send the memo, write it. It will build your confidence, and maybe you'll send it at a more opportune time. In the meantime, you can think about what you want to say in the memo, revise it, and add to it.

Whenever you have an idea that you want to be taken seriously, write a memo. It won't be long before people begin to notice that you can communicate well with written words. The ability to write well is a skill that will help you not only in business, but in many other areas of your life.

GRAMMAR IQ FINAL EXAM

Based on your work in *Grammar Essentials,* choose the best answer. Check the answers at the end of the exam.

1. Which of the following words is a spoken, rather than a written, version of a word?
- **a.** because
- **b.** should have
- **c.** until
- **d.** sorta

2. Which of the sentences below is an example of colloquial language?
- **a.** Harry got sick of his job.
- **b.** Benson postponed the meeting.
- **c.** Julie will arrive ahead of schedule.
- **d.** Bonnie needs additional time.

3. Which sentence contains an active voice verb?
- **a.** The agenda was prepared by the assistant.
- **b.** Andreas frosted the cake.
- **c.** Bilias was welcomed by the staff.
- **d.** The officials were criticized bitterly.

4. Which of the following word groups is a sentence fragment?
- **a.** After work, we met for coffee.
- **b.** They passed the bend in the road.
- **c.** And looked around for a familiar face.
- **d.** The missionaries went from door to door.

5. Which of the following fragments is a dependent clause?
- **a.** When it started to rain.
- **b.** I began to run.
- **c.** I thought she looked familiar.
- **d.** He had lost weight.

6. Which of the following fragments is a phrase without a subject or predicate?

a. Even though the agreement had been signed.
b. If she left before the half was over.
c. While the spaghetti was cooking.
d. Willing to consider another option.

7. Which of the following is a run-on sentence?

a. The electricians arrived before they were scheduled.
b. Muriel needed some space she had just suffered a terrible tragedy.
c. After we sign the papers, the house will be ours.
d. He'll have to insulate the house; otherwise, the heating bills will be enormous.

8. Choose the correctly punctuated sentence below.

a. The mail was late, consequently, the package did not arrive on time.
b. The mail was late consequently, the package did not arrive on time.
c. The mail was late; consequently, the package did not arrive on time.
d. The mail was late consequently the package did not arrive on time.

9. Choose the correctly capitalized sentence below.

a. As we Traveled down Interstate 90, we could see the Black Hills rising in the distance.
b. As we traveled down interstate 90, we could see the Black hills rising in the distance.
c. As we traveled down Interstate 90, we could see the black Hills rising in the distance.
d. As we traveled down Interstate 90, we could see the Black Hills rising in the distance.

10. Choose the correctly capitalized sentence below.
- **a.** Mrs. Baptiste moved her store, The Silver Fox, to 345 Grand Avenue in West Palm Center, Florida.
- **b.** Mrs. Baptiste moved her store, The silver Fox, to 345 Grand Avenue in West palm Center, Florida.
- **c.** Mrs. Baptiste moved her store, The Silver Fox, to 345 Grand Avenue in west Palm Center, Florida.
- **d.** Mrs. Baptiste moved her Store, The Silver Fox, to 345 Grand Avenue in West Palm Center, Florida.

11. Which of the following sentences has the correct end mark?
- **a.** How nice of you to see us;
- **b.** How nice of you to see us?
- **c.** How nice of you to see us!
- **d.** How nice of you to see us.

12. Choose the correctly punctuated sentence below.
- **a.** Intrigued, Cortez turned to ESPN, his favorite TV channel.
- **b.** Intrigued Cortez turned to ESPN, his favorite TV channel.
- **c.** Intrigued, Cortez turned to ESPN his favorite TV channel.
- **d.** Intrigued Cortez turned to ESPN his favorite TV channel.

13. Choose the correctly punctuated sentence below.
- **a.** After the meeting was over Alan who was late in the first place wanted to reconvene.
- **b.** After the meeting was over, Alan, who was late in the first place, wanted to reconvene.
- **c.** After the meeting was over, Alan who was late in the first place wanted to reconvene.
- **d.** After the meeting was over Alan, who was late in the first place, wanted to reconvene.

14. Choose the correctly punctuated sentence below.

a. Imelda visited her tailor, her cobbler her hairdresser and her accountant.

b. Imelda visited her tailor her cobbler, her hairdresser, and her accountant.

c. Imelda visited her tailor, her cobbler, her hairdresser, and her accountant.

d. Imelda visited her tailor her cobbler her hairdresser and her accountant.

15. Choose the correctly punctuated sentence below.

a. The players prepared well, for the tournament on December 20 2005 but performed poorly.

b. The players prepared well, for the tournament on December 20, 2005 but performed poorly.

c. The players prepared well, for the tournament on December 20, 2005, but performed poorly.

d. The players prepared well for the tournament on December 20, 2005, but performed poorly.

16. Choose the correctly punctuated sentence below.

a. The bus has left; you need to find another ride to the hotel.

b. The bus has left, you need to find another ride to the hotel.

c. The bus has left, you need to find another ride, to the hotel.

d. The bus has left; you need to find another ride, to the hotel.

17. Choose the correctly punctuated sentence below.

a. At 12:30 P.M. the plane, which stops at Kansas City, Kansas, St. Louis, Missouri, Dallas, Texas, and Corpus Christi, Texas, will be leaving Fort Dodge, Iowa.

b. At 12:30 P.M. the plane which stops at Kansas City Kansas St. Louis Missouri Dallas Texas and Corpus Christi Texas will be leaving Fort Dodge Iowa.

c. At 12:30 P.M., the plane, which stops at Kansas City, Kansas; St. Louis, Missouri; Dallas, Texas; and Corpus Christi, Texas, will be leaving Fort Dodge, Iowa.

d. At 12 30 P.M., the plane which stops at Kansas City, Kansas; St. Louis, Missouri; Dallas, Texas; and Corpus Christi, Texas; will be leaving Fort Dodge, Iowa.

18. Choose the correctly punctuated sentence below.

a. You need a new fuel pump; otherwise, your engine is in danger of overheating.

b. You need a new fuel pump, otherwise, your engine is in danger of overheating.

c. You need a new fuel pump, otherwise; your engine is in danger of overheating.

d. You need a new fuel pump, otherwise your engine is in danger of overheating.

19. Choose the correctly punctuated sentence below.

a. Estaban called the new book a "gift to busy students.

b. Estaban called the new book a "gift to busy students."

c. Estaban called the new book, a gift to busy students.

d. Estaban called the new book, a "gift to busy students."

20. Choose the correctly punctuated sentence below.

a. "Where did you put the mayonnaise, my mother asked. I can't find it anywhere."

b. "Where did you put the mayonnaise," my mother asked. "I can't find it anywhere."

c. "Where did you put the mayonnaise? my mother asked. "I can't find it anywhere."

d. "Where did you put the mayonnaise?" my mother asked. "I can't find it anywhere."

21. Choose the correctly punctuated sentence below.

a. I read my literature assignment, the story Incident at Owl Creek while I watched ER, my favorite TV show.

b. I read my literature assignment, the story "Incident at Owl Creek," while I watched "ER," my favorite TV show.

c. I read my literature assignment, the story "Incident at Owl Creek" while I watched "ER" my favorite TV show.

d. I read my literature assignment, the story "Incident at Owl Creek," while I watched ER, my favorite TV show.

22. Choose the correctly punctuated sentence below.

a. After the security guard's performance was evaluated, management decided to give her two weeks' severance pay and dismiss her.

b. After the security guards performance was evaluated, management decided to give her two weeks' severance pay and dismiss her.

c. After the security guard's performance was evaluated, management decided to give her two weeks severance pay and dismiss her.

d. After the security guard's performance was evaluated, management decided to give her two week's severance pay and dismiss her.

23. Choose the sentence below that uses dashes and other punctuation correctly.

a. If youre not too busy—and I know everyone is—please read and complete this questionnaire.

b. If you're not too busy—and I know everyone is—please read and complete this questionnaire.

c. If youre not too busy, and I know everyone is, please read—and complete this questionnaire.

d. If you're not too busy, and I know everyone is, please read—and complete this questionnaire.

24. Choose the correctly punctuated sentence below.

a. Al sells women's shoes at his mother-in-law's expensive ladies' store.

b. Al sells women's shoes at his mother-in-law's expensive ladys' store.

c. Al sells womens' shoes at his mother-in-law's expensive lady's store.

d. Al sells womens' shoes at his mother-in-law's expensive ladys' store.

25. Choose the correctly punctuated sentence below.

a. The secretary treasurer recorded all fifty five minutes of the hard nosed negotiations.

b. The secretary-treasurer recorded all fifty-five minutes of the hard-nosed negotiations.

c. The secretary treasurer recorded all fifty five minutes of the hard nosed negotiations.

d. The secretary-treasurer recorded all fifty five minutes of the hard-nosed negotiations.

26. Choose the correct sentence below.

a. The two-page letter of complaint took Linda 2 hours to write.

b. The 2 page letter of complaint took Linda 2 hours to write.

c. The two-page letter of complaint took Linda two hours to write.

d. The two page letter of complaint took Linda two hours to write.

27. Choose the correctly punctuated sentence below.

a. Missy reported that her mojo (what kind of word is that anyway) wasn't working.

b. Missy reported that her mojo (What kind of word is that anyway?) wasn't working.

c. Missy reported that her mojo (what kind of word is that anyway?) wasn't working.

d. Missy reported that her mojo, what kind of word is that anyway, wasn't working.

Choose the correct form of the word in parentheses in the following sentences.

28. Mid was sure the problem (is, was, am) (solve, solving, solved).

29. I believe he is (refer, refers, referring, referred) to the old contract, which has been (nullify, nullifying, nullified).

30. Marilyn (wish, wishing, wishes) that they (will, would) never (of, have) moved from their old neighborhood.

31. Eric (pay, paid) the bill and (keep, kept) the receipt.

32. The plumber (do, did, done) a complete estimate for us so that we would (know, knew, known) exactly how much the job (costed, costs, would cost).

33. The sweater (shrink, shrank, shrunk), even though I (use, used, had used) cold water.

34. My grandfather was very thrifty; he never (through, threw, throw) anything away if he thought he could (used, use, uses) it again.

35. By the time Jenna (meets, met) her fiancé, I had already (am, been, was) married for three years.

36. I learned that the earth (revolves, revolved) around the sun when I was in kindergarten.

37. If I (was, were) you, I would (took, takes, take) him up on his offer.

38. Half of the guests (was, were) late, but each of the hostesses (was, were) on time.

39. Neither the coach nor the players (want, wants) to practice this weekend.

40. Everybody wants (his or her, their) name on the trophy, but both Jon and Tom (want, wants) only (their, his) initials.

41. (We, Us) teachers wasted (fewer, less) hours than (they, them).

42. The paper is (lying, laying) on the dining room table, and the car is (setting, sitting) in the drive.

43. (Its, It's) time for a break when the day reaches (its, it's) end.

44. (Your, You're) the one (that, who, which) responds to my requests.

45. (Their, There, They're) hoping to close (their, there, they're) mortgage if the paperwork is (their, there, they're) in the office by morning.

46. (Fewer, Less) people attended the conference this year, even though there was a greater (amount, number) of key speakers than last year.

47. As it (passed, past), we watched the (plain, plane) (brake, break) slowly and stop.

48. I (hear, here) that the (hole, whole) department is required to (meat, meet) in the conference room tomorrow morning.

49. What (affect, effect) will the consultant's (advice, advise) have on (weather, whether) or not we (loose, lose, loss) more profits this year (than, then) we did last year?

50. The mayor (use, used) to think that the chief of police was (suppose, supposed) to attend all fires in the city.

ANSWERS

1. d.
2. a.
3. b.
4. c.
5. a.
6. d.
7. b.
8. c.
9. d.
10. a.
11. c.
12. a.
13. b.
14. c.
15. d.
16. a.
17. c.
18. a.
19. b.
20. d.
21. b.
22. a.
23. b.
24. a.
25. b.
26. c.
27. b.
28. was, solved
29. referring, nullified
30. wishes, would, have
31. paid, kept
32. did, know, would cost
33. shrank, had used
34. threw, use
35. met, been
36. revolves
37. were, take
38. were, was
39. want
40. his or her, want, their
41. We, fewer, they
42. lying, sitting
43. It's, its
44. You're, who
45. They're, their, there
46. Fewer, number
47. passed, plane, brake
48. hear, whole, meet
49. effect, advice, whether, lose, than
50. used, supposed

TWO-WORD VERBS

The English language is full of two-word verbs: verb-preposition combinations that are used in place of a single verb. These can be especially confusing for non-native speakers. Each sentence that follows uses a verb-preposition combination. The combinations are bolded and then defined in the parentheses that follow each one. Many writers avoid these combinations, simply because they are confusing, and use the single-word equivalent instead.

The couple **broke up** (separated).
The elevator **broke down** (stopped working) this morning.
They unexpectedly **broke off** (stopped) this relationship.
Competition **brings out** (reveals) his best work.
I hate to **bring up** (raise) such a touchy subject.

Lawrence and Stacy **called off** (canceled) their engagement.
The governor **called up** (summoned) the National Guard.

Please call if anything **comes up** (arises).
Tell us how the game **came out** (ended).

Elizabeth doesn't **care for** (like) green beans.

It won't be long before they **catch up to** (overtake) us.
Tamara **catches on** (learns) quickly.

Doris **filled out** (completed) the application.
Paige **filled up** (filled) the car with gas.
Janet will **fill in** (cover) for me this afternoon.

See if you can **find out** (discover) her birth date.

Billy should **get along** (manage) fine without our help.
Beverly hates to **get up** (arise) in the morning.
Loren **gets away** (goes undiscovered) with everything.
Becky **gets out of** (avoids) work whenever she can.
Get rid of (Discard) this extra lumber.

The losing army finally **gave up** (surrendered).
We don't **give out** (dispense) that kind of information.

The troops will **head out** (leave) in the morning.
Sandy will **head up** (lead) the committee.

I **help out** (assist) whenever I can.

Morris couldn't **hold in** (contain) his disappointment.
The doctors don't **hold out** (promise) much hope.
The strike **held up** (delayed) production.
Don't **leave out** (omit) any of the details.

Gordon will **look into** (examine) this problem.
Doug tried to **look up** (locate) the information.
Older siblings often **look after** (tend, protect) younger ones.
Since the rain, things are **looking up** (improving).

The pilot could barely **make out** (see) the runway lights.
Make out (complete) a grocery list for me.
The thieves **made off with** (took) over two thousand dollars.
The witness **made up** (invented) the story.

Mrs. Henderson is **open to** (considering) your suggestion.
Eventually, the suspect began to **open up** (reveal).

Don't **pass up** (overlook) this opportunity.
The old vicar **passed away** (died).
The singer **passed out** (fainted) from fright.

We expect you to **put forward** (expend) your best effort.
Alex sometimes **puts off** (postpones) his homework.
The boys tried to **put out** (extinguish) the fire.
It's hard to **put up with** (tolerate) incompetence.

Felix **ran across** (discovered) some interesting information.
I'm tired of **running after** (chasing) this ghost of an idea.
These chips will **run out** (be consumed) before we ever start eating.

I think I'll **sit out** (rest) during the next match.
This product should **stand up** (last) under extreme heat.
Why don't you **stand up for** (defend) yourself?

His daughter **takes after** (resembles) him.
Take apart (disassemble) this clock and see why it won't work.

We don't like it when you **talk down** (condescend) to us.
Sam likes to **talk around** (avoid, bypass) the real issue.

Will they **turn down** (reject) our request?
A computer virus can **turn up** (arise) at any time.
I think I'll **turn in** (retire) for the night.

My time and money is all **used up** (consumed).

The wolf **walked into** (entered) the trap.
Don't **walk out** (leave) on us now!

We'll try to **work around** (avoid) the obstacles.
Let's **work out** (resolve) our differences.
I'll **work up** (develop) a proposal for you.
See if the dentist can **work** me **in** (schedule me) this afternoon.

Write down (record) everything you remember from that conversation.
Can you **write in** (include) a clause about late payment?

APPENDIX B: ADDITIONAL RESOURCES

Using this book is just the first step toward becoming a better writer. If you want to learn more, you can. If you have Internet access, you can use one of the many online writing labs. If you learn better from direct instruction, many high schools and colleges offer inexpensive writing courses for adults in their communities. You may even be able to find a teacher willing to tutor you for a modest fee. If you want to strike out on your own, this appendix includes a list of books and websites you'll find helpful, as well as a little information about each one.

Books

1001 Pitfalls in English Grammar (Barron's)

- A problem-solving approach to writing and grammar; very useful for non-native speakers of English.

English Made Simple by Arthur Waldhorn and Arthur Ziegler (Made Simple Books)

- Designed for non-native speakers of English; also good for native speakers with little grammar background.

Errors in English and How to Correct Them by Harry Shaw (HarperCollins)

- Addresses specific problems in both writing and grammar; useful for non-native speakers of English.

Grammar: A Student's Guide by James R. Hurford (Cambridge University Press)

- Thorough coverage of parts of speech, sentence structure, usage, punctuation, and mechanics; especially good for native speakers of English.

The Handbook of Good English by Edward D. Johnson (Washington Square Press)

- A well-organized, comprehensive handbook for both grammar and writing.

Improve Your Writing for Work by Elizabeth Chesla (LearningExpress)

- Focuses on the larger aspects of writing—stating and supporting your main idea, organizing your thoughts, writing introdutions and conlusions—for workplace writing such as memos and reports.

Living in English: Basic Skills for the Adult Learner by Betsy J. Blusser (Contemporary Publishing Company)

- Specially designed for non-native speakers of English.

Practice with Idioms by Ronald E. Feare (Oxford University Press)

- For non-native speakers of English.

Smart English: The Easy-to-Use, Instant Access Guide to Proper Written and Spoken English by Anne Francis (Signet)

- A thorough general-purpose handbook for both writing and grammar; good for non-native speakers of English.

Thirty Days to Better English by Norman Lewis (Signet)

- Useful for general information; for both native and non-native speakers of English.

Writing Smart by Marcia Lerner (Princeton Review)

- Good for general writing skills; well organized so information is easy to find.

Websites

www.aitech.ac.jp/~iteslj/quizzes/

- Self-study quizzes for ESL speakers/writers, covering slang, holidays, reading, culture, writing, grammar, idioms, vocabulary. Helpful links to other websites.

www.LearningExpressFreeOffer.com

- FREE access to exercises designed to strengthen your grammar skills. Receive immediate scoring and detailed answer explanations.

Notes

Notes

Notes

Notes

Special Offer from LearningExpress!

Let LearningExpress help you acquire practical, essential grammar skills FAST

Go to the LearningExpress Practice Center at www.LearningExpressFreeOffer.com, an interactive online resource exclusively for LearningExpress customers.

Now that you've purchased LearningExpress's *Grammar Essentials* skill-builder book, you have **FREE** access to:

- **Forty exercises covering ALL VITAL GRAMMAR SKILLS**, from capitalization and punctuation, to subject-verb agreement and word usage
- Immediate scoring and detailed answer explanations
- Benchmark your skills and focus your study with our **customized diagnostic report**
- Improve your knowledge of important grammar rules

Follow the simple instructions on the scratch card in your copy of *Grammar Essentials*. Use your individualized access code found on the scratch card and go to www.LearningExpressFreeOffer.com to sign in. Start practicing your grammar skills online right away!

Once you've logged on, use the spaces below to write in your access code and newly created password for easy reference:

Access Code: ______________________ Password: ________________________